DR. GARY SMALLEY

Bestselling Author of *The Language of Love*

TED CUNNINGHAM

AS LONG AS
We Both
SHALL LIVE

STUDY GUIDE

Experience the Marriage You've Always Wanted

Regal

From Gospel Light
Ventura, California, U.S.A.

Published by Regal
From Gospel Light
Ventura, California, U.S.A.
www.regalbooks.com
Printed in the U.S.A.

Rights for publishing this book outside the U.S.A. or in non-English languages are
administered by Gospel Light Worldwide, an international not-for-profit ministry.
For additional information, please visit www.glww.org, email info@glww.org, or write to
Gospel Light Worldwide, 1957 Eastman Avenue, Ventura, CA 93003, U.S.A.

CONTENTS

INTRODUCTION

The *As Long as We Both Shall Live Study Guide* is designed to be used in conjunction with the *As Long as We Both Shall Live* book and DVD. Whether you take part in the study with your spouse, a small group or a church seminar, we encourage you to share what you're learning with those closest to you! Talk about the questions and Scripture passages with your spouse, friends and any mentors. As you grow closer to God and your spouse throughout the study, don't be shy about sharing the good news of what God is doing in your life.

Each section begins with an introductory section "For Starters" followed by some open-ended questions designed to get the discussion going. After you complete this section, you'll want to watch the DVD and see Gary and Ted share their thoughts and insights on the material. Then it's time for the main "Study and Discussion." You'll want to keep your Bible nearby; there are lots of great Scriptures and questions to reflect on and discuss. Finally, you'll have the opportunity to apply what you have learned through "Put It into Practice."

Our hope and prayer for you is that God will use this study to awaken new levels of communication, understanding and forgiveness in your relationship with your spouse and that you will discover the marriage you never thought possible!

THE EXPECTATIONS OF MARRIAGE

Chapter 1 in *As Long as We Both Shall Live*

Do you remember when you and your spouse were first dating? Can you remember how you felt during those first few times together? The sense of excitement and anticipation? Those butterflies fluttering in your stomach? As you began discussing what a life together might look like, you probably shared your hopes and dreams. You may have discussed your careers, your ideas of family life and countless details of what life together could look like.

If you're recently engaged, then you may be experiencing some of those moments right now! But if you've already taken your vows, then odds are you've had front-row seats to see how all the expectations are playing out. Even if you couldn't express them, you've seen your expectations coming to the surface. Expectations like where you were going to live, what you were going to do together, and what life was going to be like have probably been sources of great discussion and maybe even some disagreement.

Now that you're married, life has turned out a little (or a lot!) different than you expected. Your idea of married life may have been a million miles from what you've actually experienced. And you may have found yourself frustrated, discouraged or disappointed from time to time. If so, know that you are not alone!

Every bride and groom enters marriage with a list of expectations—some spoken, but most unspoken—about what life together is going to look like, feel like and be like. Yet, a few days or weeks into the marriage, many of these expectations are still unfulfilled. Why is this such a big deal? Because of the way this can play out in a relationship. As the years pass, unmet expectations can lead to greater disappointment and even disillusionment. If left unchecked, emotions of anger and resentment can lead to withdrawal from each other until eventually a couple may be tempted to separate.

Gary and I have both seen this play out in a marriage. The progression looks something like this:

The Progression of an Unhealthy Marriage

Unmet Expectations ➡ Disillusionment ➡ Disconnect ➡ **Divorce**

Unfortunately, this is happening in far too many marriages in America. The good news is that this doesn't have to be the outcome of yours! You can begin doing things today that will not only increase the health, satisfaction and joy in your marriage but will also help you and your spouse become a model and inspiration to countless other couples.

What does the progression of a truly healthy marriage look like?

The Progression of an Healthy Marriage

Unmet Expectations ➡ Discovery ➡ Personal Responsibility ➡ **Commitment**

In other words, it's natural and normal for some expectations to go unmet in a marriage. Your spouse was simply not designed to meet all of your needs and desires. Only God can do that! Once you recognize the expectations in your life that are unmet, then you can study them and discover where they come from and how you can take personal responsibility for your own actions and beliefs. As you do, you'll find yourself developing healthy expectations for yourself and your spouse that lead to a fulfilling marriage commitment.

So whether you're engaged, newly wed or you've been married for more years than you can count, this study is designed to strengthen your marriage to be all that God intended! We can't wait to take this journey with you.

For Starters

Think of several expectations about marriage that you can look back on and laugh about when you think of them now. In the space below, describe three of those expectations you no longer have.

_____

_____

_____

_____

_____

Think of several expectations about marriage that you had on your wedding day and still have today. In the space below, list three of them.

_____

_____

_____

_____

_____

What is the difference between the expectations you now consider as silly and those you consider as reasonable and timeless? How would your marriage be different if you held on firmly to those silly expectations? How would your marriage be different if you let go of those reasonable expectations?

_____

_____

_____

_____

_____

_____

Introduction to DVD

Everyone walks into marriage with some expectations. Some of those expectations are healthy and good, but others are unreasonable or even harmful for the relationship. In this first lesson, we're going to explore the great expectations of marriage. You will be challenged to reflect on the expectations you brought into your marriage and how your relationship is measuring up. Along the way, you'll begin to discover how you can better deal with the unmet expectations in your marriage and life. Let's watch as Gary and Ted introduce this idea.

Discussion and Study

It's important to recognize that expectations are not a bad thing! We believe that everyone should come into marriage with expectations—like expecting that you and your spouse will remain faithful to each other; that you will remain committed for a lifetime; that you will grow more in love as the years pass. These are good and healthy expectations! But how you deal with your expectations when they go unmet can impact your spiritual, mental and emotional health.

Can you think of any healthy expectations that can help strengthen a marriage . . . other than the ones described in the paragraph above? Describe those expectations in the space below.

_____

_____

_____

_____

_____

_____

Can you think of any unhealthy expectations that can undermine a marriage? Describe them in the space below.

_____

_____

_____

_____

_____

_____

Think about an expectation you had early in your relationship that went unmet. How did you respond? In the space below make a list of some of the emotions you felt as a direct response to your unmet expectation.

_____

_____

_____

_____

_____

How did you resolve the issue of unmet expectations in this area of your marriage? Or has it remained unresolved? Explain in the space below.

_____

_____

_____

_____

_____

We want to help you move beyond any unhealthy or unrealistic expectations and into an abundant, life-giving marriage where your needs are met and your dreams are realized. This kind of transformation doesn't happen overnight. That's why in the upcoming study, Gary and I are going to dive into the Scriptures to see where men and women have wrestled with expectations in their marriages, in their lives and in their relationship with God. In addition, we want to share stories from our lives as well as the lives of those we know and counsel.

Jacob's Unmet Expectations

Jacob was a man familiar with unmet expectations when it came to marriage. From the day he laid his eyes on his bride-to-be, Rachel, his life was wildly different than he ever could have imagined.

Read Genesis 29:1-11. How did Jacob respond to meeting Rachel (see vv. 10-11)?

_____

_____

_____

_____

_____

Though the Scripture does not specifically say, what do you think was going through Jacob's mind, heart and emotions during his first encounter with Rachel (see vv. 10-11)?

_____

_____

_____

_____

_____

_____

Read Genesis 29:12-20. What was Laban's response to Jacob?

_____

_____

_____

_____

_____

Following Laban's initial response, what do you think some of Jacob's expectations were regarding his relationship with Rachel?

_____

_____

_____

_____

_____

Even during the seven years of service, Jacob was a man who was madly in love. The Scripture says that those years seemed like just a few days because of his affection for Rachel. Yet all of the expectations and anticipation that Jacob stored up during those seven years were dashed in a single event.

Read Genesis 29:21-26. How did Laban deceive Jacob?

_____

_____

_____

_____

_____

How do you think Jacob's expectations regarding marriage were affected?

_____

_____

_____

_____

Read Genesis 29:27-30. How did Laban offer to resolve the situation? Do you think the offer was fair? Why or why not? Why do you think Laban tricked Jacob?

_____

_____

_____

_____

At their first encounter, Jacob was smitten with Rachel. Over the years of service to his future father-in-law, Jacob developed all kinds of expectations of what his life with Rachel would look like. Instead, he ended up with two wives—Rachel and Leah—and the conflict and struggle had only just begun.

Read Genesis 29:31-35. After Jacob married Rachel, what kind of unexpected conflict arose in their marriage?

_____

_____

_____

_____

_____

Reflecting on Genesis 29, Jacob had all kinds of great expectations of what marriage would look like. Yet his life turned out more different than he ever could have anticipated.

The Gap Between Expectations and Reality

Every person experiences a gap between his or her expectations and reality when it comes to marriage. Think about your own wedding vows. If you used traditional vows, then you made the promise to stay committed for better and worse, whether rich or poor, in sickness and in health. Consider the gap between expectations and actual experience.

What You Experienced	What You Expected
Worse	Better
Poor	Rich
Sickness	Health
End of Marriage	Marriage for a Lifetime

What is the gap? The gap is the difference between what you pictured in your mind and what reality is. The gap is the difference between what you imagine and what is real. The gap is the difference between your expectations and your experiences. The wider the gap between the expectation and the experience, the more strain in a marital relationship.

The Gap and the Strain

What You Experienced . . . . What You Expected

For Jacob, the gap between what he expected and what he experienced was like a gigantic gorge. He felt the strain and tension in his home every day—it was reflected in his relationship with his wives and eventually his children.

In what ways has your life turned out different from what you expected? How has this affected your attitude toward your spouse? Your family? Your marriage?

_____

_____

_____

_____

_____

The Great Expectations Quiz

In The Great Expectations Quiz, we have listed 78 common expectations for marriage. As you read through the list, we want to challenge you to go deeper than just saying "Yes, that's me, I have that expectation." Instead, ask yourself, "How strong is this expectation?" Remember, the greater the intensity of the expectation, the more distant it is from reality.

Rank the expectations you brought into your marriage. On a scale of 1 to 10, 1 being "not a big deal," and 10 being "I totally expected that," rank the expectations behind your vows. For example, if you planned on holding hands every day for the rest of your life, you would probably give that a 10. If holding hands was not a big deal, but you enjoyed it from time to time, you may give yourself a 5. If you didn't like holding hands or it was not that important to you, give yourself a 1. We want you to rank the intensity or strength of the desire for each expectation.

On a scale of 1 to 10, place a number on the left side of the statement that represents what you expected in your marriage in this area. On a scale of 1 to 10, on the right side of the statement rank your experience in your marriage. Keep in mind that we are looking for the gaps, because the gaps are what cause the strain, disillusionment, frustration and hurt.

NOTE TO THOSE TAKING THE QUIZ

For those not yet married: Before you tie the knot, you need to get premarital counseling and/or training. As you talk through issues with a trusted pastor or leader, discuss your expectations honestly and openly. Use word pictures to describe what you long for, hope for and desire. Imagine a perfect day in marriage during your first year, your fifth year, your tenth year and your twentieth. Make sure you move beyond "We just love each other so much" to answering the deeper questions of the heart. Take "The Great Expectations Quiz" and share the score with your fiancé. Don't be afraid to be brutally honest—it will strengthen your relationship for the long haul.

For those already married: Now here is a caution: You may be tempted while reading this list to respond with, "Oh brother, you've got to be kidding me!" "Get over it!" or "Our puppy love went out the window a long time ago!" No matter how long ago you were married, go back to your wedding day. As you read through "The Great Expectations Quiz," what do you remember expecting on that day? What do you remember experiencing? Your marriage may be drifting . . . for some time; but what we are asking you to do is answer this simple question: *Did I ever have this expectation at some point in my marriage relationship?*

WHAT YOU HOPED FOR	EXPECTATION	WHAT YOU GOT
	1. We will have children. (If unable to have children, imagine the hurt and pain of a woman who wants to be a mom and her husband who wants to be a father.)	
	2. We will have many children.	
	3. We will have few children.	
	4. Long walks on the beach. (We will walk for no other purpose but connecting. Just me and my spouse, with the sand between our toes, our pants legs rolled up and the tide coming in.)	
	5. He will be a spiritual leader. (We will pray together, have daily devotions and attend church regularly.)	
	6. She will know how to submit.	
	7. Regular church attenders.	
	8. Nice house. (Imagine a white picket fence, furniture and backyard garden or downtown loft. Maybe not necessarily your first home, but your home a few years down the road.)	
	9. Romantic vacations. (Cruises, beach houses or remote cabins in the Rockies. The honeymoon experience will happen at least once a year.)	
	10. Regular vacations. (My spouse will take time away from the job or career each year to devote a full week to our marriage and family.)	

WHAT YOU HOPED FOR	EXPECTATION	WHAT YOU GOT
	11. Deep conversations. (While dating, we spent hours on the phone. There will never come a day when I sense he is "rushing" me off the phone. My spouse will always love the sound of my voice.)	
	12. Bragging on each other in public. (While dating, we talked each other up to family and friends and showed each other's picture every chance we got. This will continue throughout our marriage.)	
	13. Courtesy. (Opening doors, pushing back a chair, offering a jacket on a cold night.)	
	14. Kindness. (We will always exchange uplifting, positive words in our communication.)	
	15. Give up friends. (I know that once we get married, my spouse will no longer have a desire to spend prolonged periods of time with friends. Hanging out with me will trump hanging out with friends.)	
	16. Time with friends. (My spouse will let me enjoy plenty of time with my friends. After all, we need relationships outside of the marriage to make life rich.)	
	17. Great eye contact. (When I speak, everything will stop because what I have to say will be treasured. My spouse will remove all distractions and focus on me.)	
	18. Hand holding. (We will hold hands at all times, in the movies, in the car, at the mall, during church and even at home.)	
	19. Patience. (We will never grow tired of repeating ourselves when the other person does not understand what we are saying.)	
	20. Dress up for dates and special nights. (My spouse will always put some thought into what he/she is wearing when we date.)	

WHAT YOU HOPED FOR	EXPECTATION	WHAT YOU GOT
	21. We won't change. (*Our personalities and passion will not fade or change with time.*)	
	22. Dates. (*From eating out to movies, we will have a regular date night that nothing interferes with.*)	
	23. The "I'm glad to see you" look. (*When we get home from work, there will always be an overwhelming response of elation to being in each other's presence.*)	
	24. Media will not consume our time. (*Our television viewing will be limited to a show/sporting event or two a week.*)	
	25. Freedom from addiction. (*Substance abuse, alcohol, pornography will not destroy our marriage.*)	
	26. Unconditional love. (*My spouse will love me even when I am going through difficult times emotionally.*)	
	27. Physical health. (*We will remain healthy throughout our marriage. Caring for each other through major illness will not be necessary.*)	
	28. Tenderness/gentleness. (*Our words will defuse anger and encourage each other.*)	
	29. Validation. (*My spouse will always understand my fear, frustration or hurt. Listening to me will always triumph over trying to solve my problems.*)	
	30. Together forever. (*We will never leave each other. The "D" word—divorce—will never be an option for us. We are together until one of us lays the other in the arms of Jesus.*)	

WHAT YOU HOPED FOR	EXPECTATION	WHAT YOU GOT
	31. *Snuggling on the couch. (Movie nights with popcorn will be a regular occurrence. Sometimes we will just snuggle with nothing to watch on TV. Just enjoying each other's presence will be enough.)*	
	32. *Sharing feelings. (I will always know my spouse's dreams, goals, hurts, hang-ups and frustrations. I will never have the need to guess, because there will always be a free flow of information.)*	
	33. *Grace and forgiveness. (The spirit of forgiveness will always exist in our home. We will not judge because we each are imperfect and make mistakes. There will be plenty of room for error.)*	
	34. *Devotions and prayer. (We will have a regular, daily quiet time with each other. We will work through the Bible, a book or devotional. We will pray at every meal.)*	
	35. *Cleanliness. (My spouse will always maintain a clean space, be it the closet, office, family room or bedroom. My spouse will always pick up and clean up his/her stuff.)*	
	36. *Closeness vs. close by. (We will always have a connectedness. We will never have the "in the same room, but checked out mentally" home.)*	
	37. *Humor/lightness. (We will never take ourselves too seriously. We know when to lighten up and when to laugh at ourselves.)*	
	38. *Servant, butler or maid. (We will cherish the opportunities to serve one another. We will always be that couple that refills an empty glass or picks up the dirty clothes of the other. Without hesitation or frustration we will look for opportunities to serve each other.)*	

WHAT YOU HOPED FOR	EXPECTATION	WHAT YOU GOT
	39. Home-cooked meals. (*My spouse will have the table set, dinner on the stove and even, at times, candles lit. Dinner out or ordered in will be infrequent. Meals will be as good as [or better than] my mom's.*)	
	40. Understanding of work pressure. (*We will work hard to give each other space at the end of a long day.*)	
	41. Appreciation for work, job and career. (*My spouse will show interest in what I do and what I contribute to the family's bottom line.*)	
	42. Eyes for no other; faithfulness. (*My spouse's "eyes" do not wander off of me and onto another.*)	
	43. Ease of the words "I'm sorry." (*Remember when you were first dating? When you would offend one another, not only did the apology come easily, but often it was repeated.*)	
	44. Admission of mistakes. (*My spouse will always be forthcoming with mistakes and character defects in his/her life.*)	
	45. Appreciation for hobbies. (*I will have no problem with the time required for my spouse's hobbies, and my spouse will have no problem with mine.*)	
	46. Cared for when sick. (*Did he or she prepare get-well baskets stuffed with tissue, soup, candles or a favorite magazine? That kindness will continue throughout our marriage.*)	
	47. United front. (*No one will ever be able to put me down to my mate. No parent, family member or friend would get away with slandering me to him/her.*)	
	48. Protection. (*My spouse will take a bullet for me if necessary. Sounds in the middle of the night will be quickly investigated and resolved.*)	

WHAT YOU HOPED FOR	EXPECTATION	WHAT YOU GOT
	49. Companion. (We will love doing things together. We will never be one of those couples that go their separate way at movies, the mall or even at church.)	
	50. Sleeping together. (We will never sleep in separate rooms.)	
	51. Sex every day. (Regular sex will solve any lust problems.)	
	52. Creative sex. (Now I have the context to explore my sexual fantasies.)	
	53. Quickies. (She will serve me even when she is not in the mood.)	
	54. Sex all night. (We will make love until the sun comes up. Multiple orgasms will be experienced often.)	
	55. Family. (We will love each other's family and friends.)	
	56. Fondness of parents. (We will both get along well with our parents.)	
	57. Mom and Dad. (My spouse will like to hang around my mom and dad.)	
	58. Family history. (My spouse will show compassion for my family history.)	

WHAT YOU HOPED FOR	EXPECTATION	WHAT YOU GOT
	59. Accepting my family. (We will not judge or be critical of the actions of each other's family.)	
	60. Time with extended family. (My spouse will love spending a lot of time with my family members.)	
	61. In-law visits once or twice a year. (Mom and Dad will be able to set healthy boundaries without us needing to tell them. Visits will be minimal to help us "leave and cleave.")	
	62. Family holidays. (My spouse will have no problem with my family taking control of the holidays.)	
	63. Family traditions. (My spouse will happily honor my family traditions around the holidays.)	
	64. Decisions. (My spouse will have no problem seeing things from my point of view.)	
	65. One family income. (My spouse will make plenty of money to cover our expenses so I can stay home with the kids.)	
	66. Financial responsibility. (My mate will hold down a good job, make a good living and provide for the needs of the home.)	
	67. Financial security. (We will have plenty of money to do what we need to do as a family. We will be all about paying bills on time, keeping debt to a minimum and giving to charitable organizations.)	
	68. Financial freedom. (My spouse will have no problem spending money freely. We will not need to keep a tight rein on the checkbook.)	

WHAT YOU HOPED FOR	EXPECTATION	WHAT YOU GOT
	69. Tithing. (We will give a minimum of 10 percent of our income to our church.)	
	70. Savings. (We will spend less than 100 percent of what we make so we have some to put into savings.)	
	71. Giving. (Money will be set aside to give to charitable organizations beyond our tithing.)	
	72. Retirement. (We will have plenty of money saved up so that we can stop working at a reasonable age.)	
	73. Church denomination. (We will mutually agree on the denomination for our family. My spouse will not bash my denominational preference.)	
	74. Theology. (We will merge our beliefs and have few theological differences.)	
	75. Worship style. (We will enjoy the same kind of worship experience.)	
	76. Entertainment. (From music to movies, we will be able to find a happy medium that both of us can enjoy.)	
	77. Promptness. (We will both work to be at events and family gatherings on time.)	
	78. Physically fit. (We will live healthy lives. Excessive weight gain will not occur.)	

Much like raising the bar on a high jumper, we want to help you set new goals and challenges for your marriage. When you have positive expectations, your marital skills can and most likely will rise to the challenge. We want to help you establish realistic expectations while also challenging you to sharpen your skills as a spouse. This will help you bridge the gap between your expectations and your actual experience in marriage.

The Key to Narrowing the Gap

We believe the key to narrowing the gap between your expectations and your experiences is found in your own heart. You alone are responsible for your attitudes, actions and reactions. The good news is that you don't have to make this journey alone. God is with you, and through Him anything is possible! Nothing is beyond redemption. Need proof? Let's revisit the story of Jacob.

Though the culture and practices described in ancient times may seem unusual to the modern reader, go ahead and read Genesis 30:1-24. Jacob probably imagined having a large family with many sons who would help protect, guard and care for the family and their livestock. He never imagined having two wives both wrestling with infertility at different times and competing to have children through the surrogacy of their maids. Furthermore, as if being deceived by your father-in-law into marrying a woman you didn't really love, struggling with infertility and competition between two wives and their maids were not enough, Jacob's marital challenges were also compounded by the conflict with his wives' family.

Read Genesis 30:25-43; 31:1-2. Why was Laban at odds with Jacob?

_____

_____

_____

_____

What happened to Laban's attitude toward Jacob (see v. 2)?

_____

_____

_____

_____

Read Genesis 31:1-21. How did God intervene in the situation (see vv. 3,9,11-12,16)?

_____

_____

_____

_____

_____

Even when Jacob was on the run from his father-in-law, God was still with him and protecting him. Read Genesis 31:22-55. How do things turn out for Jacob and his family?

_____

_____

_____

_____

_____

Though Jacob had countless expectations that were not met in his marriage and family life, it was clear that God's hand was on Jacob's life. And Jacob was obedient in his relationship with God. When things seemed too difficult, God's presence and direction were key to getting through the tough times and fulfilling the calling and destiny on Jacob's life. Though it wasn't always clear in the darker moments, God was faithfully pursuing a relationship with Jacob.

On the way back to his homeland, Jacob encountered a stranger he wrestled with until daybreak. Refusing to let the stranger go, Jacob held on and stubbornly declared, "I will not let you go unless you bless me!" During that encounter, which is described in Genesis 32, Jacob was given a new name: Israel. He had wrestled with God and men, and prevailed.

This story is a welcome reminder that no matter what you may be wrestling with in your marriage and your life, God is with you. He goes before you. And He will prepare a way out that will protect you and your family and bring you into the land of blessing and promise He has intended for you all along.

Taking It with You

All of us will encounter moments in our personal relationships when our experiences do not meet our expectations. The question is how will you respond? Will you allow yourself to be swallowed by disillusionment and disappointment, or will you view the moment as an opportunity for discovery?

The Progression of a Healthy Marriage

Unmet Expectations ➡ Discovery ➡ Personal Responsibility ➡ **Commitment**

God wants your marriage to grow into the healthiest marriage possible. By studying your expectations and taking them to God in prayer, you can be better prepared to close the gap between your expectations and reality and experience a more joy-filled marriage.

Put It into Practice

Choose at least one of the suggested activities below to complete over the next week. Consider sharing the results with your friends or small-group members. Tell them about the impact this activity has had on you and your relationship with your spouse.

1. Reflect on Your Great Expectations Quiz Results

Now that you've taken the Great Expectations Quiz, take a few moments to reflect on the results. Do you see any patterns among your answers? Are there any themes to the areas where you seem to be most satisfied or frustrated? Spend some time prayerfully considering each area of success and struggle.

2. Study Yourself and Your Spouse

Over the course of the next week, pay special attention to any hot-button areas where tempers flare, or moments when either you or your spouse are tempted to withdraw. How are these areas of conflict tied into your expectations? Can you identify any expectations that are fueling these conflicts? Are there any underlying issues that you and your spouse need to discuss?

3. Pray for Your Spouse

Take at least 15 minutes today to pray for your spouse. But during the entire time of prayer, don't ask God to change your spouse. Ask God to reveal what changes need to happen in your heart so you can better love, support and encourage your spouse. Take every opportunity over the next week to fulfill any opportunities to love your spouse no matter what.

DEEP ROOTS AND CULTURAL INFLUENCES

Chapters 2–3 in *As Long as We Both Shall Live*

Have you ever thought about the source of your expectations for your marriage, family and life? The roots of your expectations may go deeper than you think! That's why in this session we're going to move to the second stage in the progression of a healthy marriage.

The Progression of a Healthy Marriage

Unmet Expectations ➡ Discovery ➡ Personal Responsibility ➡ **Commitment**

The journey to discovery begins in your childhood and goes all the way back to the way you were raised. Whether you realize it or not, your parents (or those who raised you) have had a tremendous effect on how you see the world and what you expect out of life. Whether you grew up with two parents, one parent, an extended family member or foster care, you came out of the womb with eyes and ears that filmed and audiotaped every experience. When you were learning to speak, you weren't just learning words. You were learning tones and nuances and facial expressions. When you were sitting in the backseat of the car on a trip, you weren't just going on a family excursion, you were picking up cues as to what marriage, parenting and a family should look like.

Now fast-forward a few decades. You're married, and maybe you even have a family of your own. Though you're now sitting in the front seat of the car, you're still trying to reconcile what you experienced as a kid to what you're experiencing now. What is a family supposed to look like? What does it mean to be a good mom or dad? What do you want to make sure your kids get that maybe you never got? All of these are good questions to ask, but if you'll look closely, you'll notice that they're all laced with expectations—those great expectations of what life could or should look like.

In the next few sessions we're going to take you on a journey of discovery. We want to challenge you to not only recognize the expectations you've brought into your marriage, but more importantly, to understand where they come from. In this session, we're going to look at two sources of expectations: our families and our culture. While very different from each other, both have the power to shape the way we see the world and interact with our spouse.

For Starters

Spend a few moments thinking about your childhood and your family. What are three things you loved about the way you were raised that you'd like to give to your own children? Describe in the space below.

_____

_____

_____

_____

Can you think of one thing you would do differently in raising your own children? Describe.

_____

_____

_____

_____

_____

In what specific ways do you think our culture influences the way you think about marriage and family? Do you think those influences are primarily healthy, unhealthy, or benign? Explain.

_____

_____

_____

_____

_____

Introduction to DVD

The formation of the expectations you bring into marriage may go back further than you think. The way you were raised, the culture you engaged in and the generation you were born in all influence the way you view marriage. In this second lesson, we're going to explore some of the roots of what has shaped your expectations. Along the way, you'll better understand where your expectations are coming from. We believe that when you understand your past, you're in a better position to shape your future. Let's watch as Gary and Ted introduce this idea.

Discussion and Study

Did you know that most parents raise their children in one of four basic parenting styles? That's amazing to consider! But there are four primary styles of parenting.

Four Primary Parenting Styles

The Dominant Parent. Dominant parents have expectations for their children. They want their kids to excel in every area and they're willing to do whatever it takes to make sure their child succeeds. They often have stiff rules in place to make sure any unnecessary obstacles don't trip up their child. Unfortunately, they often fail to explain the reasoning behind these rules, so the child may secretly participate in unwanted behavior anyway.

In the space below, place a checkmark by any comments you frequently heard while growing up:

_____ Rules are rules. No exceptions.

_____ You don't need reasons. Just do what I say.

_____ I don't care how many of your friends will be there. You're not going, and I don't want to hear another word about it, do you hear?

_____ You committed to this, so there's no backing out.

On a scale of 1 to 10, how do you feel the Dominant Parent describes the way you were raised?

1	2	3	4	5	6	7	8	9	10
Not Dominant at All									Extremely Dominant

The Neglectful Parent. Neglectful parents often show an uncaring or immature attitude. These parents tend to isolate themselves from their children by excessive use of baby-sitters and indulging in their own selfish activities. Children are viewed as a bother "to be seen and not heard." Neglectful parents aren't around a lot, so kids spend a lot of time alone as they grow older.

In the space below, place a checkmark by any comments you frequently heard while growing up:

_____ Can't you see I'm busy?

_____ You can't stay up. You wanted to stay up late last night. Stay out of my hair!

_____ That's your problem. I've got to get to work.

_____ Good grief! Can't you be more careful?

On a scale of 1 to 10, how do you feel the Neglectful Parent describes the way you were raised?

1	2	3	4	5	6	7	8	9	10
Not Neglectful at All									Extremely Neglectful

The Permissive Parent. Permissive parents are often their children's friends' favorite parents. They tend to be warm, supporting people, but weak in establishing and enforcing rules and limits for their children. They are often willing to host the neighborhood party for kids but leave the youth unsupervised. Often, permissive parents are afraid they may damage their children or lose their kids' love if they are too strict. As a result, children of permissive parents may get away with vandalism, bullying or substance abuse.

In the space below, place a checkmark by any comments you frequently heard while growing up:

_____ Well, okay, you can stay up late this time. I know how much you like this program.

35

_____ I hate to see you under all this pressure from school. Why not rest tomorrow? I'll say you're sick.

_____ Please don't get angry with me. You're making a scene.

_____ Please try to hurry. I'll be late again if we don't get going soon.

On a scale of 1 to 10, how do you feel the Permissive Parent describes the way you were raised?

1	2	3	4	5	6	7	8	9	10
Not Permissive at All									Extremely Permissive

The Loving and Firm Parent. Loving and firm parents often have clearly defined rules, limits, and standards for living. They take time to train their children to understand these limits—like why we don't break people's stuff and what to do when accidents happen. They provide clear warnings when a child has transgressed an established limit. This is balanced with lots of expressions of verbal and physical affirmation as well as time together. The loving and firm parent is a healthy and balanced combination of the Dominant Parent and the Permissive Parent.

In the space below, place a checkmark by any comments you frequently heard while growing up:

_____ You're late again for dinner, Tiger. How can we work this out together?

_____ Hey, I wish I could let you stay up later, but we agreed on this time. Remember what you're like the next day if you miss your sleep?

_____ When we both cool off, let's talk about what needs to be done.

_____ You're really stuck, aren't you? I'll help you this time. Then let's figure out how you can get it done yourself next time.

On a scale of 1 to 10, how do you feel the Loving and Firm Parent describes the way you were raised?

1	2	3	4	5	6	7	8	9	10

Not Loving and Firm at All   Extremely Loving and Firm

Knowing Your Roots

As you look at the list of parenting styles below, which did you most experience as a child? Place a check by the one that best describes the way you were raised. Now place a check by the one that best describes the way your spouse was raised.

_____ The Dominant Parent

_____ The Neglectful Parent

_____ The Permissive Parent

_____ The Loving and Firm Parent

How has that experience shaped you? How has it shaped your spouse?

_____

_____

_____

_____

_____

_____

How has that experience shaped your expectations of marriage and family? Your spouse's expectations of marriage and family?

_____

_____

_____

_____

_____

How have your roots affected the way you're growing into a spouse, parent and follower of Christ? How have your spouse's roots affected him or her in these roles?

_____

_____

_____

_____

_____

No matter what style of parenting you were raised under, the Bible makes it clear that we are to honor our mother and father. Honoring does not mean condoning unbiblical behavior. It does not mean passing on any of the unbecoming qualities of our parents to our children. But it does mean choosing to remember the good things over the bad. This is so important to God that it's listed as one of the Ten Commandments.

Read Exodus 20:12. What commandment is highlighted in this verse?

_____

_____

_____

_____

According to the second half of the verse, why is it so important to follow this commandment? What happens to someone who refuses to honor his or her father and mother?

_____

_____

_____

_____

Have you ever known someone whose unresolved relationship with his or her mother or father actually seemed to hold the person back in life? If so, explain.

_____

_____

_____

_____

Is there anything in the past with your own relationship with your mom or dad that needs to be forgiven so that you can move forward into the "land which the Lord your God gives you" (Exodus 20:12)? Explain.

_____

_____

_____

_____

_____

Shaped by the Generations

In addition to being influenced by the way you were raised, you are also shaped by the generation in which you were born. This isn't a topic many people dive into, but we believe it's key to helping identify some of the sources of marital conflict as well as some of the conflict you experience in everyday life.

As part of the Builder Generation, (a person born between 1922 and 1943), I've been amazed to discover that few people today know to stop for funeral processions. I remember the day when people pulled off to the side of the road and stopped for a funeral as a sign of respect. But today, the world doesn't work that way.

Recently, I was attending a funeral and riding in the front seat of the hearse. I'm usually fairly patient, but watching people speed in front of a hearse irritated me to no end. I turned to the driver and asked, "Is this normal?"

"Yeah, it is now," he answered. "Nobody has time anymore. We're all going so fast."

At one point during the procession, we needed to make a left turn where there wasn't a light. More than 20 cars passed in oncoming traffic before I stepped out of the hearse, stepped into traffic and held up my hand for people to stop. Finally, someone stopped so the funeral procession could continue.

My expectations about respect for a funeral procession come directly from the generation into which I was born. The historical events and culture surrounding my generation shaped the way we respond to things like funeral processions. They also mold and shape the expectations I brought into marriage.

For example, the Builder Generation is known for never allowing divorce as an option. Meanwhile, a Boomer is more likely to marry, stay married for a long time and then divorce. A buster will marry quickly, divorce quickly and then marry again quickly. Bridgers are delaying marriage and waiting for compatibility with someone they identify as their soul mate. Every generation is different and each one brings different expectations into marriage.

The Four Generations

As you read about the characteristics of these generations, keep in mind that you may have some characteristics from a generation other than your own. For instance, I (Gary) am a Builder, but I take on many of the characteristics of a Boomer. Ted is a Buster, but after hanging around him for many years, I have noticed Boomer tendencies in him. Maybe that is why we get along so well.

Generation No. 1: Builders

Born: 1922–1943

Defining Events: The Great Depression and World War II

Values: Hard work, law and order, respect for authority, duty, loyalty and honor

Marital Expectations: Stay married, work through issues, work hard

Generation No. 2: Baby Boomers

Born: 1943–1960

Defining Events: The civil rights movement, invention of the television, post World-War II rebuilding

Values: Health and wellness, personal growth, involvement, efficiency

Marital Expectations: Longevity in marriage, mask marital expectations to maintain the façade of perfection, work hard and long for success

Generation No. 3: Busters

Born: 1960–1980

Defining Events: Watergate, the fall of the Berlin Wall, the rise
of MTV

Values: Diversity, global thinking, pragmatism

Marital Expectations: Marriage deserves a chance, divorce is
always an option, work as much as needed

Generation No. 4: Bridgers

Born: 1980–now

Defining Events: September 11, 2001, Columbine shootings,
invention of the Internet, popularity of reality TV

Values: Freedom of choice, flexibility, authenticity, creativity

Marital Expectations: Delay marriage; wait for compatibility in
a soul mate; work smarter rather than harder

As you look at the list of generation styles below, which describes you?
Now place a checkmark by the one that best describes your spouse.

____ The Builder Generation

____ The Boomer Generation

____ The Buster Generation

____ The Bridger Generation

In what ways has the generation you were born into shaped your expectations for marriage? Your expectations for raising a family?

_____

_____

_____

_____

_____

The Cultural Factor

In addition to having your expectations shaped by your parents and your generation, you are also being molded by the culture around you. Music, television, movies, books, the Internet, theater performances and other cultural elements are constantly shaping the way you view life.

What is your favorite romantic movie? Why is it your favorite? What about the plot, the storyline or the characters do you love the most?

_____

_____

_____

_____

_____

Think about the perfect marriage. What popular song would you select as a theme song for that marriage?

_____

_____

_____

_____

What book have you read recently that best describes what a great marriage looks like?

_____

_____

_____

_____

_____

What cultural element—music, television, movies, books, the Internet, theater—most influences the way you think about marriage and family?

_____

_____

_____

_____

While many movies and television programs depict beautiful moments of sacrifice, loyalty and faithfulness in marriage, there are many that tarnish the view of what marriage is designed to be. Do you think it's important to focus your time and energy on shows, movies and music that offer a healthy view of marriage? Why or why not?

_____

_____

_____

_____

In the space below, write the words of Philippians 4:8:

_____

_____

_____

In the space below, write the words of Psalm 119:37:

_____

_____

_____

Read Isaiah 33:14-16. According to this passage, what is required of the person who is to dwell with God (see v. 15)?

_____

_____

_____

_____

What is promised to the person who does those things (see v. 16)?

_____

_____

_____

_____

Culture may try to sway you with all kinds of arguments and persuasive ideas that simply don't represent God's best for your life. Here are four choruses we frequently hear throughout culture:

Chorus No. 1: "It's Mine; All Mine"
Chorus No. 2: "It's All About Me"
Chorus No. 3: "If It Feels Good, Do It"
Chorus No. 4: "To Each His Own"

Of those four choruses, which are you most susceptible to "singing"?

_____

_____

_____

_____

Which one is most likely to undermine your marriage?

_____

_____

_____

_____

_____

_____

What can you do to protect your marriage, your spouse and your family from falling prey to these cultural choruses?

_____

_____

_____

_____

_____

_____

Scripture calls us to be separate from the world but not isolated from it. How do we do that? We live in culture while guarded and filtered through God's agenda by spending time studying the Scriptures, talking with God (praying) throughout the day, spending time with fellow believers and committing to grow together with our spouse.

Taking It with You

Your expectations have roots! Whether you're influenced by the way you were raised, the generation you were born into or the culture in which you live, your view of marriage and family is being shaped by influences outside yourself. The good news is that by recognizing what is shaping your expectations, you can take personal responsibility for the way you live and relate to others and prayerfully allow God to shape your expectations into healthy ones. You don't have to be influenced; you can become an influencer. You can begin fighting for your marriage and family. You can start setting down standards of godliness, including showing more love, compassion and hope. You can make the decision that marriage is forever and commit to never allowing divorce to be an option. You can begin enjoying the marriage God designed for you to have all along.

Put It into Practice

Choose at least one of the activities suggested below to complete over the next week. Consider sharing with your friends or small-group members the impact it has on you and your relationship with your spouse.

1. Reflect on Your Roots

Spend some time prayerfully considering the way you were raised. What parenting style did you experience? What did you like about it? What did you not like? Make time this week to talk with your spouse about the differences in the ways both of you were raised and how you want to raise and influence your children and grandchildren.

2. Review Your Movie and Music Collections

Take a look at the DVDs that you have on your shelf as well as your CDs and music downloads. Which are your favorites? What kind of messages are they communicating about love, godliness and your relationship with your spouse? Are they encouraging you to be all that God has created you to be, or are they tarnishing that image? Spend some time this week enjoying music and movies that encourage you to live as God intended!

3. Memorize a Scripture Passage

This week commit the following Scripture to memory: "Finally, brothers, whatever is true, whatever is noble, whatever is right, whatever is pure, whatever is lovely, whatever is admirable—if anything is excellent or praiseworthy—think about such things" (Philippians 4:8).

PERSONALITY PLAY AND UNPACKING PAST RELATIONSHIPS

Chapters 4–5 in *As Long as We Both Shall Live*

Do you realize how uniquely and wonderfully you've been made? God designed you to be different from every other person on the entire planet. Need proof? Just look at your fingertips. No other person has the exact same design in his or her fingerprints. Amazing, isn't it?

Your uniqueness isn't found only when you look in the mirror or at your fingerprints; it's also found internally. God made you with certain likes and dislikes, preferences and desires. He even gave you your own personality—complete with all kinds of colorful quirks that your spouse has probably discovered by now!

Odds are good that your personality is much different from your spouse's. You probably respond to situations and people differently. You may even look for solutions to everyday problems in completely different ways. One of the beautiful things about marriage is that it's often the differences that initially attract two people to each other. But other times, if one or both spouses lose sight of appreciating these differences, they can become a source of conflict. That's why it's so important to know the way you're wired and the way your spouse is wired. Understanding how your personality comes into play in any given situation goes a long way to helping establish healthy boundaries and patterns in a marriage.

Chances are that if you've been experiencing conflict or frustration in your marriage, it's a direct result of not understanding how God made your spouse. That's why in this session we're going to explore the four personality types. We'll examine how understanding personalities can help bring your expectations into line in your marriage relationship and lead you into a more fulfilling relationship.

For Starters

Make a list of three things that you absolutely love and appreciate about your spouse. Then make a list of three things that you wish you could change about your spouse.

LOVE AND APPRECIATE	WISH YOU COULD CHANGE

Now take a step back and look at your lists. Which entries are linked to personality differences?

_____

_____

_____

_____

_____

_____

Do you see any connection between your spouse's greatest strengths and greatest weaknesses? Do you see any connection between your own strengths and weaknesses? Explain.

_____

_____

_____

_____

Introduction to DVD

Your personality is always at play in your relationships. Whether you realize it or not, you tend to respond to certain people and situations in a particular way. So does your spouse! In this session, we're going to examine the four types of personalities and how they influence the expectations you bring into marriage. Let's watch as Gary and Ted introduce this idea.

Discussion and Study

God made you unique and He designed you perfectly! When it comes to who you are, God did not make a mistake. The psalmist recognized this simple but powerful truth when he wrote: "For you created my inmost being; you knit me together in my mother's womb. I praise you because I am fearfully and wonderfully made; your works are wonderful, I know that full well" (Psalm 139:13-14).

How does it make you feel to know that God created your "inmost being" and knitted you together in your mother's womb?

_____

_____

_____

_____

Do you believe that God did a good job when He made you? Why or why not?

_____

_____

_____

_____

_____

_____

Is there anything that prevents you from accepting the truth that you are "fearfully and wonderfully made"? If so explain.

_____

_____

_____

_____

_____

_____

Do you feel like you know the truth of Psalm 139:13-14 "full well"? Why or why not?

_____

_____

_____

_____

_____

_____

The Four Personality Types

There are four personality types, but most likely you are a blend of one or more of them. And your spouse is too! Read through the four personality types to determine which describes you the most:

The Precise Personality (aka the Beaver Personality). The Precise Personality loves analyzing, statistics, measuring and comparing things. This personality tends to see things in black or white and is ready to play the role of critic.

PRECISE PERSONALITY	
Relational Strengths:	Accuracy and precision Assures quality control Discerning Analytical
Strengths Out of Balance:	Too critical or too strict Too controlling Too negative of new opportunities Loses overview
Communication Style:	Factual Two-way Great listener (tasks) Weakness: Desire for detail and precision can frustrate others Quality
Relational Needs:	Exact expectations
Relational Balance:	Total support is not always possible Thorough explanation isn't every- thing

Precise Personality expectations:
- Let's do everything right and in order
- Let's be on time to appointments and family events
- Give me ALL the details in the conversation

- Don't lie about the facts (I just say I'm leaving out some details so the story is more interesting)

The Pleaser Personality (also known as the Golden Retriever). The Pleaser Personality is warm, relational, calm and loyal. This personality wants to make sure that everyone and everything is good.

PLEASER PERSONALITY	
Relational Strengths:	Warm and relational Loyal Enjoys routine Peacemaker Sensitive to others' feelings Attracts the hurting
Strengths Out of Balance:	Missed opportunities Stays in a rut Sacrifices own feelings for harmony Easily hurt or holds a grudge Indirect Two-way
Communication Style:	Great listener Weakness: Uses too many words or provides too many details Emotional security
Relational Needs:	Agreeable environment Learn to say no—establish emotional boundaries
Relational Balance:	Learn to confront when your feel- ings are hurt

Pleaser Personality expectations:
- Let's do everything together
- Let's meet each other's needs
- Let's have plenty of conversations
- Let's stay in harmony

The Party Personality (also known as the "Otter"). The party personality is all about fun, laughter and having a good time. The party personality is the life of the party and wants to make sure that everyone is enjoying themselves.

PARTY PERSONALITY	
Relational Strengths:	Optimistic Energetic Motivators Future oriented
Strengths Out of Balance:	Unrealistic or daydreamer Impatient or overbearing Manipulative or pushy Avoids details or lacks follow- through
Communication Style:	Can inspire others Optimistic or enthusiastic One-way Weakness: High energy can manipu- late others Approval
Relational Needs:	Opportunity to verbalize Visibility Social recognition Be attentive to mate's needs
Relational Balance:	There is such a thing as too much optimism

Party Personality expectations:
- Let's have fun with whatever we are doing
- Let's not be too serious
- We must learn to laugh at ourselves

The Powerful Personality (also known as the Lion). The Powerful Personality is a decisionmaker who wants to get things done. Task oriented, he or she is prone to leadership positions and quick to tackle projects.

POWERFUL PERSONALITY	
Relational Strengths:	Takes charge Problem solver Competitive Enjoys change Confrontational
Strengths Out of Balance:	Too direct or impatient Too busy Cold blooded Impulsive or takes big risks Insensitive to others
Communication Style:	Direct or blunt One-way Weakness: Not always a good listener
Relational Needs:	Personal attention and recognition for what they do Areas where he or she can be in charge Opportunity to solve problems Freedom to change Challenging activities Add softness
Relational Balance:	Become a great listener

Powerful Personality expectations:
- Let's get it done
- Let's do it my way
- Give me just enough details in the conversation

As you look at the list of personality types below, which describes you? Now place a checkmark by the one that best describes your spouse.

_____ The Precise Personality

_____ The Pleaser Personality

_____ The Party Personality

_____ The Powerful Personality

In what ways does your personality complement your spouse's personality?

_____

_____

_____

_____

In what ways does your personality create opportunities for conflict with your spouse's personality?

_____

_____

_____

_____

What changes can you make to help strengthen the communication, compassion and understanding when it comes to personality differences in your marriage?

_____

_____

_____

_____

One of the most incredible things about personality differences is that God uses every different personality type to accomplish and fulfill His purposes and build His Kingdom. Consider the story of two sisters: Mary and Martha. Both were raised in the same family yet their personalities couldn't have been more different from each other!

Read Luke 10:38-42. How did Martha respond to Jesus' visit?

_____

_____

_____

_____

_____

How did Mary respond to Jesus' visit?

_____

_____

_____

_____

_____

Reflecting on the four personality types—Precise, Pleaser, Party and Powerful—which would you say best describes Martha?

_____

_____

_____

_____

_____

Which would you say best describes Mary?

_____

_____

_____

_____

_____

It's all too easy to wrap up reading Luke 10 and think that Martha had a lot to learn while her sister seemed to make the better decisions of simply being with Jesus. But this passage is just a snapshot of Martha and Mary's relationship with Jesus. In the Gospel of John we read of another encounter of the two sisters and Jesus.

Read John 11:1-37. What caused the sisters to send a message to Jesus (see John 11:1)?

_____

_____

_____

_____

_____

Upon Jesus' arrival, what did He discover (see John 11:17)?

_____

_____

_____

_____

_____

How was Martha's response to Jesus' arrival different from Mary's? How does this reflect the difference in their personalities (see John 11:20)?

_____

_____

_____

_____

_____

_____

How does Martha display her faith in her interaction with Jesus (see John 11:21-27)?

_____

_____

_____

_____

_____

It's interesting to note that one of the most often quoted Scriptures was a direct result of Martha interacting with Jesus. Through her dialogue with Christ, we are given one of the most profound declarations of faith: "I am the resurrection and the life. He who believes in me will live, even though he dies; and whoever lives and believes in me will never die" (John 11:25-26).

In confidence, Martha responds: "Yes, Lord," she told him, "I believe that you are the Christ, the Son of God, who was to come into the world" (John 11:27). Then, she is the one who goes back and calls to her sister Mary to let her know that Jesus wants to see her.

How did Mary respond to the invitation of Jesus (see v. 29)?

_____

_____

_____

_____

_____

What was Mary's response to Jesus compared to Martha's (see John 11:21-22,32)? How did the differences in their responses reflect their personalities?

_____

_____

_____

_____

Read John 11:28-43. How would the story have been different if only Mary or Martha were present? How is the story and the faith journey of all strengthened by the presence of Mary and Martha?

_____

_____

_____

_____

One of the amazing things about learning to appreciate different personalities is that not only do we learn things about ourselves that we could not learn any other way, but we also discover things about God—who He is and who He has created us to be.

Celebrating Personality Differences in Marriage

So how do you turn personality conflict into celebration?

First, accept the personality difference. Recognize that God has made you different from your spouse in order to strengthen you!

Read Ecclesiastes 4:7-12. According to this passage, what are some of the benefits of being with someone else?

_____

_____

_____

_____

_____

Being with someone else can strengthen and empower you. In good times and bad, you have someone with you who can guard, protect, encourage and help you along the way. Now this is where personality differences are an extra blessing. Think about it. If you were just like your spouse, you would not only share the same strengths, but you would also share the same weaknesses. So when the storms of life come, both of you would be more likely to be harmed. Your differences are actually your strength as a couple!

Read Romans 15:7. What is the result of accepting your spouse just as he or she is?

_____

_____

_____

_____

_____

_____

Second, avoid judging or criticizing personality differences. It's easy to find fault with a personality that's different from your own, but the Bible challenges us to extend love, compassion and kindness to others.

Read Matthew 7:1-5. What instruction is given toward judging others?

_____

_____

_____

_____

Why do you think it's easier to see the speck of sawdust in someone else's eye rather than the plank of wood in your own?

_____

_____

_____

_____

Third, allow for misunderstandings and trial and error. Even the best marriages have misunderstandings. Often the conflict that results can be compounded by personality differences. At those moments, it's important to look for ways to build each other up and not tear each other down.

Read Proverbs 12:18. What wisdom does this verse offer for moments of tension in marriage?

_____

_____

_____

_____

Read Ephesians 4:2. What attitude should you have as you deal with misunderstandings?

_____

_____

_____

_____

_____

Remember that you and your spouse have personality differences—and that's a good thing! Learn to celebrate the differences and expect to grow together in love and appreciation for those differences.

Unpacking the Boxes of Past Relationships

As you learn to celebrate each other's personalities, you may also discover another source that is shaping your expectations for marriage: your past relationships. Whether you married the first person you dated or can't possibly keep count, it's important to realize that your previous relationships can influence and impact the expectations you've brought into your marriage. As you unpack the boxes of previous relationships, here are a few things to keep in mind:

Unpack the box with help from others. A trained counselor, pastor, trusted friend or small group are invaluable resources when you're dealing with your past relationships. You need someone to talk to. You need someone to help you process the effect of past relationships. And you need someone to help you walk in wisdom. The people who help you along this journey should be wise, godly counselors.

The good news is that unpacking the box is not something you have to do on your own. In John 14:16, Jesus said, "I will ask the Father, and he will give you another Counselor to be with you forever." Do you know who that "Counselor" is? It's the Holy Spirit. The word used in Greek is *Paraklesis,* meaning "to come alongside to encourage." In other words, as you unpack the boxes in your life, God's Spirit is with you every step of the way.

So prayerfully invite God's Spirit to illuminate areas of woundedness and hurt from the past. Ask Him to expose the areas that still need to be renewed and redeemed. And remember that no matter what you're going through, you are not alone. God is with you!

Let your spouse be a part of the unpacking. Please be sensitive to this. You do not need to share every detail of every "item" in your past relationships box, but you can share tidbits to allow your spouse to glean more insight into the expectations you brought with you. You can use the unpacking as an opportunity to not only heal and restore your past, but also build a stronger, healthier future.

Sort through your expectations. Categorize your expectations as if you were getting ready for a garage sale. Some expectations you have brought into marriage are good. Others just need to be pitched. How do you tell the difference? You need to prayerfully take your expectations to God.

In John 7:24, Jesus instructed, "Stop judging by mere appearances, and make a right judgment." You cannot make righteous judgments apart from God's wisdom and insight. He is the one who sees the hidden things of the heart and helps us identify those things that are true and good and just. Ask Him for His wisdom.

Don't repack. Once you have unpacked the past, don't return to your old behavior or sins. This is a foundational part of true repentance and change. Consider for a moment the story of one woman who had a closet full of boxes to unpack from her previous relationships:

Early in the morning He came again into the temple, and all the people were coming to Him; and He sat down and began to teach them. The scribes and the Pharisees brought a woman caught in adultery, and having set her in the center of the court, they said to Him, "Teacher, this woman has been caught in adultery, in the very act. Now in the Law Moses commanded us to stone such women; what then do You say?" They were saying this, testing Him, so that they might have grounds for accusing Him.

But Jesus stooped down and with His finger wrote on the ground. But when they persisted in asking Him, He straightened up, and said to them, "He who is without sin among you, let him be the first to throw a stone at her." Again He stooped down and wrote on the ground.

When they heard it, they began to go out one by one, beginning with the older ones, and He was left alone, and the woman, where she was, in the center of the court. Straightening up, Jesus said to her, "Woman, where are they? Did no one condemn you?"

She said, "No one, Lord."

And Jesus said, "I do not condemn you, either. Go. From now on sin no more'" (John 8:2-11, *NASB*).

Can you imagine the forgiveness and love in Jesus' eyes? Can you sense the firmness in His voice when He said, "From now on sin no more" (v. 11)? No matter what is in your past, nothing is beyond God's redemption and restoration. But moving forward truly does require letting go of the past.

Taking It with You

Your expectations for marriage are often shaped by your personality. Whether your personality is defined by the characteristics of the Precise, Pleaser, Party, or Powerful personality, God made you perfectly! He wants to use you to encourage and bless others—including your spouse. Odds are that your spouse's personality is completely different from your own. And that's a good thing. Your differences actually make you a stronger, more dynamic couple, and that's something to treasure and celebrate.

Meanwhile, depending on your past, you may have boxes that you still need to unpack. You may have expectations from previous dating relationships or even a previous marriage. The good news is that nothing is beyond God's ability to forgive, redeem and renew. You can begin developing healthy expectations for the future today.

Put It into Practice

Choose at least one of the suggested activities below to complete over the next week. Consider sharing with your friends or small-group members the impact it has on you and your relationship with your spouse.

1. Take a Formal Personality Test with Your Spouse

You may have taken a personality test (DISC, Birkman or another kind) at work; but have you taken a personality test at home with your spouse? Sometimes the things you uncover and discover about yourself can help you get along with others more successfully. You may see things about yourself you've never seen before. And your spouse can do the same. If taken in a loving, encouraging atmosphere, a personality test can be a tool to draw you closer together, improve your communication with each other and better understand the expectations you have for your marriage.

2. Go Out of Your Way to Be Kind to Someone Different from You

Reflect on the four personality types and look for the one that is most different from yours. Now think about all the people in your life—in your neighborhood, work and community. Is there someone who tends to get on your nerves or drive you crazy? Prayerfully consider some specific ways you can bless and encourage that person this week. Share your personal journey with your spouse and discuss what you learn along the way.

3. Memorize a Scripture Passage

This week, commit the following Scripture to memory: "For you created my inmost being; you knit me together in my mother's womb. I praise you because I am fearfully and wonderfully made; your works are wonderful, I know that full well. My frame was not hidden from you when I was made in the secret place. When I was woven together in the depths of the earth, your eyes saw my unformed body. All the days ordained for me were written in your book before one of them came to be. How precious to me are your thoughts, O God! How vast is the sum of them!" (Psalm 139:13-17).

SESSION 4

EXPECTING THE BEST AND EXTRAVAGANT LOVE

Chapters 6–7 in *As Long as We Both Shall Live*

Over the last few sessions we've invited you into a place of discovery when it comes to the source of your expectations. We've challenged you to look at your roots and the way you were raised. We've asked you to look at your personality and how it affects your marriage, as well unpack the boxes of previous relationships. Now that you recognize some of the influences that are shaping your expectations, we are going to move to the third stage in the progression of a healthy marriage.

> **The Progression of a Healthy Marriage**
>
> Unmet Expectations → Discovery → Personal Responsibility → **Commitment**

We want to introduce you to the idea of personal responsibility and challenge you to take full responsibility for your expectations, no matter what the source. Now that you've looked at where your expectations come from, it's important to step back and align them with reality.

Proverbs 13:12 offers a simple but profound truth: "Hope deferred makes the heart sick." The idea is that when we don't get what we hope for, over time our heart will sour. We will be prone to bitterness, anger and a short temper. That's why it's so important to examine what you're putting your hope in. Is it your spouse? Your family? Your home? Your work? Your future?

In this world there is only one safe place to place your hope . . . that place is God! God alone is the one who can satisfy us and meet every need. He will use people to meet those needs. But we are never to substitute people as the source of fulfillment. Remember that God gives us relationships to enrich our lives, not to be our lives.

That's why in this session we're going to challenge you to realign your expectations and close the gap between what you expect and what you experience. You will be challenged to do that by learning to love extravagantly. Truly, love covers a multitude of sins and shortcomings. And love helps ensure that your marriage becomes all that God designed it to be.

For Starters

In the space below, make a list of three expectations you brought to marriage that have the widest gap between what you expected and what you have experienced in your relationship with your spouse.

1. _____

2. _____

3. _____

Do you think that your expectations are fair and reasonable? Why or why not?

_____

_____

_____

_____

_____

If you expressed each of the three expectations to your spouse, do you think your spouse would find them reasonable? Why or why not?

_____

_____

_____

_____

Introduction to DVD

When it comes to your expectations in marriage, you—and no one else— are 100 percent responsible for them. That's why it's so important to take a good look at your expectations and make sure they're healthy and reasonable. You may need to make some changes in your attitude in order to realign your expectations. In the process, it's important to keep your eyes on God and ask for His help. Remember, God is the one who strengthens you with His love. Let's watch as Gary and Ted introduce this idea.

Discussion and Study

How do you take personal responsibility for your expectations? You begin by realigning your expectations with reality. And only YOU can do that! This first exercise is designed to help you realign your expectations.

In the space below, make a list of the expectations you've brought into your marriage that you still hold on to even though they have gone unmet. Prayerfully ask the Holy Spirit to expose your expectations—those spoken and unspoken.

_____

_____

_____

_____

Now you need to address each expectation one at a time. Prayerfully ask God to reveal where these expectations came from and whether or not they are reasonable to keep. Are there any adjustments you need to make to your list of expectations to make them more attainable? If so, make a list of your newly modified expectations below:

_____

_____

_____

_____

_____

Now, reviewing your original list again, are there any expectations that you need to eliminate completely? If so, write them below and then draw a line through each one, symbolically marking it out. Then spend time in prayer asking God to change your heart regarding this expectation.

_____

_____

_____

_____

_____

Finally, take another look at your original list. Are there any expectations that are unreasonable or unbiblical? Open your Bible and read 1 Corinthians 13. Do each of your expectations fit within the guidelines of this Scripture passage? If so, write the remaining expectations below.

_____

_____

_____

_____

_____

Through this exercise, some of your expectations may have been modified or even eliminated. It's amazing how looking at our expectations through God's eyes can change us. The healthiest list of expectations you can have for yourself is not based on what you can get from your spouse but on what you can give to your spouse. That's why it's important to start a new list of expectations we have for ourselves to give to our mates. Take a few moments to read 1 Corinthians 13:4-7. In the space below, write out 1 Corinthians 13 in regards to your relationship with your spouse.

Example: (Insert your name) *is patient toward* (insert your spouse's name). (Insert your name) *is kind toward* (insert your spouse's name).

_____

_____

_____

_____

_____

Extravagant Love

So how do you display extravagant love to your spouse? For me (Gary), I started thinking of the love God has for me. I began meditating on the love of God and the many Scriptures that reveal His love. As I did, I began to realize that as God's child, I am to show His love to everyone I come in contact with. I can't generate one ounce of love on my own. In fact, the Bible says God is love, and we love because He first loved us (see 1 John 4:16,19).

Imagine your heart as a big tank. All too often it's easy to run around on empty. Without time spent in prayer and reading God's Word, you will run dry on God's love. But as you meditate on God and His Word, He fills you with the truth of who He is and His overwhelming love for you.

Read Romans 8:35-40. In the space below, make a list of the things that will try to separate you from the love of Christ.

_____

_____

_____

_____

What is the promise given to the children of God during these trials (see v. 37)?

_____

_____

_____

_____

Second Corinthians 5:14-17 says, "For the love of Christ controls us, having concluded this, that one died for all, therefore all died; and He died for all, so that they who live might no longer live for themselves, but for Him who died and rose again on their behalf. Therefore from now on we recognize no one according to the flesh; even though we have known Christ according to the flesh, yet now we know Him in this way no longer. Therefore if anyone is in Christ, he is a new creature; the old things passed away; behold, new things have come" (*NASB*). According to this passage, how are we changed when the love of Christ controls us?

_____

_____

_____

_____

As we recognize God's love, we are empowered to share it with others. It goes back to that picture of your heart as a tank. When it's overfilled, you can't help but pour out what's in it onto others—including your spouse.

One of the most extravagant acts of love found in the Bible was performed by a young woman who broke a jar of alabaster at Jesus' feet. Read Mark 14:1-9. What was some of the criticism the woman received for her outrageous gift?

_____

_____

_____

_____

_____

_____

What was Jesus' response to the gift (see vv. 6-9)?

_____

_____

_____

_____

_____

What is a righteous response to extravagant acts of love?

_____

_____

_____

_____

_____

Is there anything that prevents you from being more extravagant in the way you display love? Explain.

_____

_____

_____

_____

_____

What actions, words and attitudes make your spouse feel truly loved?

_____

_____

_____

_____

_____

What are some specific ways you can express extravagant love to your spouse this week?

_____

_____

_____

_____

_____

What kind words does your spouse really need to hear?

_____

_____

_____

_____

What kind words do you need to hear from your spouse?

_____

_____

_____

_____

Another small action that goes a long way is encouragement. Hebrews 3:13 challenges, "But encourage one another daily, as long as it is called Today, so that none of you may be hardened by sin's deceitfulness." In other words, we need each other to speak words of encouragement and blessing every single day! Without them, we can find our hearts growing hard toward God and soft toward complacency.

What kind of encouragement does your spouse really need right now? How can you provide it?

_____

_____

_____

_____

What kind of encouragement do you need right now that your spouse can provide?

_____

_____

_____

_____

Look for ways to love your spouse extravagantly every day!

Taking It with You

Expecting the best in your marriage means focusing on what you can give instead of what you can get. When you look for ways to love extravagantly, give outrageously and embrace wholeheartedly, you will create an atmosphere of nurture, honor and celebration in your marriage. That change doesn't begin with your spouse—it begins with you. As you prayerfully seek God and grow in your relationship with Him, you'll find your love tank filling up until you can't contain it any longer and extravagant love will naturally pour out of you!

Put It into Practice

Choose at least one of these suggested activities below to complete over the next week. Consider sharing with your friends or small-group members the impact it has on you and your relationship with your spouse.

1. Review the List

Review the list of "Unexpected, Unaffordable, Immediate Acts of Love" found on pages 156-157 of *As Long as We Both Shall Live*. The list offers more than 30 ways that you can shower your spouse with affection and affirmation. Select at least three of the activities to do this week and show your spouse just how much you appreciate and love him or her!

2. Study God's Love in Scripture

Do you want to know just how much God loves you? Then go online to a resource like biblegateway.com or crosswalk.com and type in phrases like "God's love," "love of God" and "love" in a Scripture search engine. You will be amazed at the expressions of God's love throughout the Bible and you'll be reminded of just how much He loves you!

3. Memorize a Scripture Passage

This week commit the following Scripture to memory: "For I want you to know how great a struggle I have on your behalf and for those who are at Laodicea, and for all those who have not personally seen my face, that their hearts may be encouraged, having been knit together in love, and attaining to all the wealth that comes from the full assurance of understanding, resulting in a true knowledge of God's mystery, that is, Christ Himself, in whom are hidden all the treasures of wisdom and knowledge" (Colossians 2:1-3, *NASB*).

THE SERVANT AND COMMITTED FOREVER

Chapters 8–9 in *As Long as We Both Shall Live*

My wife, Amy, knows just the right thing to say at just the right time! Often these moments happen when she and I (Ted) are lying in bed reading together. Midway through a page she will look up and share a quick word with me that blows major wind in my sail.

A few nights ago, Amy was reading a book about men. She wanted to get some insights on raising young boys and ended up learning a lot about me. The book she was reading explored the adventurous spirit men thrive on. Amy is a nester and enjoys pouring herself into her home and making it a special place for her family. I like the open road and I dream of the day when my family can pack up in an RV and spend a year traveling.

Needless to say, we have opposite ideas for our future.

Halfway through the third chapter, she put the book down and said, "Let's start looking for an RV!"

"What?!" I exclaimed.

"I never knew how important adventure was for you, and I now get it," she said.

While we didn't run out and buy an RV right away, the moment reminded me of two very important aspects of growing a healthy marriage: maintaining a servant's heart and celebrating the commitment of marriage. In those precious moments Amy and I talked, she was placing my desires above her own and demonstrating what it means to be a servant.

I'm fairly confident that RVing with kids would not be the easiest thing on her, yet she was willing to suggest and encourage the idea. Looking for an RV also reminded me of something I all too often take for granted in my marriage, and that is that my wife is committed to this relationship forever. Commitment isn't just an idea that Amy believes in; it's something that she wants to live out (and so do I). She's in this thing for the long haul, through thick and thin, through cramped quarters and the open road. Remember the progression that happens when a marriage is growing and alive:

The Progression of a Healthy Marriage

Unmet Expectations ➡ Discovery ➡ Personal Responsibility ➡ **Commitment**

Over the course of this study, we've walked through the stages of unmet expectations to discover personal responsibility. Now it's time to dive into the subject that all of this has been leading toward: Commitment. As you grow together over time, discover things about yourself and take personal responsibility for your attitude and actions, you will find yourself not just deeply committed to your spouse but committed to doing everything it takes to make the relationship thrive.

For Starters

Why do you think it's so important to maintain a servant's heart in a marriage? Why do you think it's so easy to lose a servant's heart?

_____

_____

_____

_____

What are some of the lifelong goals you share with your spouse?

_____

_____

_____

_____

_____

What activities do you and your spouse do that highlight your commitment to one another?

_____

_____

_____

_____

_____

Introduction to DVD

As you grow in taking personal responsibility for your attitudes and actions, you can't help but strengthen your marriage. The very foundation of marriage is commitment. Dreaming together, serving each other and loving each other help nurture life in you and your spouse. Let's watch as Gary and Ted introduce this idea.

Discussion and Study

Jesus' life, death and resurrection displayed the real meaning of being a servant. Though He both led and served the disciples and the multitudes that followed Him, Jesus displayed what it means to be a servant in a simple act.

Read John 13:1-17. Why was this evening so significant to Jesus and the disciples (see vv. 1-5)?

_____

_____

_____

_____

_____

What did Jesus do when He got up from the meal (see vv. 4-5)? What symbolism was displayed in His actions?

_____

_____

_____

_____

Why do you think Simon Peter protested Jesus' action (see vv. 6-9)?

_____

_____

_____

_____

_____

What lesson did Jesus want to teach His disciples through His actions (see vv. 12-17)?

_____

_____

_____

_____

In what ways do you "wash your spouse's feet" (serve your spouse) on a regular basis?

_____

_____

_____

_____

_____

_____

Are there any things you can do to be more intentional about washing the feet of your spouse on a daily basis?

_____

_____

_____

_____

_____

Are there any ways in which you're short-circuiting your spouse's efforts to serve you? Explain.

_____

_____

_____

_____

_____

_____

Washing each other's feet is only one of the many ways we are encouraged to love one another. Throughout the Bible we are given countless examples and admonitions to love and serve each other.

Read Matthew 10:42. What act of service is mentioned in this passage? Why is it so significant?

_____

_____

_____

_____

_____

_____

_____

Read Acts 20:18-20. What act of service is mentioned in this passage? Why is it so significant?

_____

_____

_____

_____

_____

_____

Read Galatians 6:10. What act of service is mentioned in this passage? Why is it so significant?

_____

_____

_____

_____

_____

_____

_____

Sometimes the issue of the roles that men and women fulfill in a marriage in regard to serving one another can cause conflict. Read Ephesians 5:22-33. Why do you think this passage can be so problematic for men and women?

_____

_____

_____

_____

What instructions are wives given in Ephesians 5:22-24?

_____

_____

_____

_____

What instructions are husbands given in Ephesians 5:25-30?

_____

_____

_____

_____

Which do you think is the more difficult assignment: the instructions given to women or the instructions given to men? Explain.

_____

_____

_____

_____

What does it mean when the Bible says "two will become one flesh" (Ephesians 5:31)?

_____

_____

_____

_____

_____

In what ways have you and your spouse "become one flesh"?

_____

_____

_____

_____

Why do you think it's so important for a man to love his wife and a wife to respect her husband (see Ephesians 5:32)?

_____

_____

_____

_____

Why does Paul prescribe love for wives and respect for husbands? In what way have you found this prescription helpful in your own marriage?

_____

_____

_____

_____

Understanding the roles in marriage is essential for developing healthy expectations. As you discuss the questions above with your spouse, you'll find yourself understanding each other's expectations better and arriving at a common agreement on how you can best serve, love and live with each other.

Healthy Expectations

When it comes to healthy expectations in a marriage, we believe there are a lot of great ones—like the roles described in the previous section. With all the expectations mentioned in the study guide, you may be tempted to reduce your expectations down to zero. You may even be tempted to think that the best expectation you can have in a marriage is no expectation at all, but we believe there are several expectations you should rank at a level 10 and keep them at that level. Here are 17 expectations you should always maintain:

1. *He will be a spiritual leader.* We will pray together, have daily devotions and attend church regularly.
2. *Bragging on each other in public.* While dating we bragged each other up to family and friends and showed our picture every chance we got. So this will continue throughout our marriage.
3. *Courtesy.* Opening doors, pushing back a chair, offering a jacket on a cold night.
4. *Kindness.* We will always exchange uplifting positive words in our communication.
5. *Patience.* We will endure with one another.
6. *Freedom from addiction.* Substance abuse, alcohol, pornography will not destroy our marriage.
7. *Unconditional love.* My spouse will love me even when I am going through difficult times emotionally.

8. *Tenderness/gentleness.* Our words will defuse anger and encourage each other.

9. *Validation.* My spouse will understand my fear, frustration or hurt. Listening to me will always triumph over solving my problems.

10. *Together forever.* We will never leave each other. The "D" word (divorce) will never be an option for us. We are together until one of us lays the other in the arms of Jesus.

11. *Grace and forgiveness.* The spirit of forgiveness will always exist in our home. We will not judge each other, because we both are imperfect and make mistakes. There will be much room for error.

12. *Devotions and prayer.* We will memorize at least 50 great verses in Scripture and meditate together daily on these verses, hearing the meaning of each verse. These verses will give us the top 10 most important beliefs within our hearts that Christ directs us to have. We will pray at every meal.

13. *Eyes for no other, faithfulness.* His eyes do not wonder off of me and onto another for prolonged lustful thoughts.

14. *Admission of mistakes.* My spouse will always be forthcoming with mistakes and character defects in his/her life. When offenses occur, my spouse will seek forgiveness from me.

15. *Cared for when sick.* Did he or she prepare get-well baskets stuffed with tissue, soup, candles or a favorite magazine? That mercy will continue throughout the years.

16. *United front.* No one would ever be able to put me down to my mate. No parent, family member or friend would get away with slandering me to him/her. We will remain in harmony and united in a win-win agreement with all arguments.

17. *Protection.* My spouse will take a bullet for me if necessary. Sounds in the middle of the night will be quickly investigated and resolved.

As you read through this list, were there any expectations that your spouse has met for you almost all the time? Describe in the space below.

_____

_____

_____

_____

_____

_____

As you read through this list, were there any expectations that you need to revive in your marriage? Describe in the space below.

_____

_____

_____

_____

_____

_____

Are there any expectations that you'd like to add to the list? Describe in the space below.

_____

_____

_____

_____

_____

The Beauty of Commitment

One of the most beautiful things about commitment is that it's not just found in marriage; it's representative of an even greater commitment: the one God has for you! God has committed to be with you until the end of time. He is faithful and true. He will never leave you nor forsake you.

Read Psalm 145:18. What is God's commitment to you in this verse?

_____

_____

_____

_____

_____

Read Matthew 18:20. What is God's commitment to you in this verse?

_____

_____

_____

_____

_____

Read Hebrews 13:5-6. What is God's commitment to you in these verses?

_____

_____

_____

_____

_____

Read 1 Corinthians 10:13. What is God's commitment to you in this verse?

_____

_____

_____

_____

_____

_____

God is faithful! Even in the hard and difficult times, God's commitment is to be with you and see you through. This commitment, which is part of His covenantal love, is a portrait of what He invites you to enjoy in your marriage—a promise to be together and grow together no matter what!

Taking It with You

Commitment grows in a marriage as you serve and love one another. When you look for opportunities to truly serve one another and celebrate the commitment of your relationship, then you create an atmosphere for deepening the bonds of an amazing marriage. As you prayerfully seek God and grow in your relationship with Him, you'll find yourself becoming more like Jesus and growing an even bigger servant's heart.

Put It into Practice

Choose at least one of the suggested activities below to complete over the next week. Consider sharing with your friends or small-group members the impact it has on you and your relationship with your spouse.

1. Read Matthew 25 and Consider the Parable of the Talents

As you prayerfully reread this parable, consider it in terms of your own marriage. Have you buried any of the talents God has given you to put to use in your marriage and/or family? How can you use the natural talents God has given you to serve your spouse? Your family? Your community?

2. Demonstrate a Servant's Heart

Over the course of the next week, look for 10 small things you can do to truly serve your spouse without any expectation of acknowledgement or even appreciation. Go above and beyond to pay attention to your spouse's desires, needs and even whims. At the end of the week, write down how these small acts of kindness affected your heart as well as your spouse's heart.

3. Memorize a Scripture Passage

This week commit the following Scripture to memory: "Instead, whoever wants to become great among you must be your servant, and whoever wants to be first must be your slave—just as the Son of Man did not come to be served, but to serve, and to give his life as a ransom for many" (Matthew 20:26-28).

A FULFILLING MARRIAGE

Chapters 10–11 in *As Long as We Both Shall Live*

My (Ted's) daughter, Corynn, age 4, still doesn't know how to handle it when I hug Amy in the kitchen when I come home. I'll be hugging her and kissing her, and Corynn will demand, "What are you doing, Daddy . . . leave her alone . . . stop!"

"It's been a long day and I'm so glad to be home," I try to explain to her. The moment she understands, she goes from trying to protect her mom to wanting in on the action! She literally tries to jump into the middle of it. So we start hugging on her and we fall on the ground together and start kissing her.

If you are married and have had children, you know the richness and joy that comes during these times in marriage. For me, being with my family is one of the most fulfilling aspects of my marriage. I can't get enough of it! And when those difficult times come—and they do—then I remember the joy and delight of those moments in the kitchen. Not only do they give me strength and hope, but they also remind me of the bigger picture, namely, the fulfilling marriage Amy and I are committed to living together.

Like Ted, Norma and I (Gary) have definitely experienced some ups and downs in our marriage. But I can tell you that we are still finding the relationship growing sweeter every day. There's something special about knowing all that we've been through, forgiven each other for, and grown through that is priceless and irreplaceable. From traveling together to serving in a ministry together, I look back in awe over the years Norma and I have been together and for all that God has done in us and through us. After all these years, I can truly say she is my best friend and the love of my life.

That's why in this final session, we want to nurture the heart of commitment in your life. A good marriage truly is one of the best parts of life and one you won't want to miss!

For Starters

List three "priceless moments" from your marriage. What made them so special?

_____

_____

_____

_____

_____

Why do you think commitment is so foundational for a healthy marriage?

_____

_____

_____

_____

_____

How does knowing that you and your spouse are committed to each other strengthen your relationship?

_____

_____

_____

_____

_____

Introduction to DVD

A marriage built on commitment has the strongest of foundations. As you learn to develop healthy expectations and nurture each other through healthy communication and compassionate understanding, you can't help but grow closer together. Let's watch as Gary and Ted introduce this idea.

Discussion and Study

In a healthy marriage, you grow together over time, discover things about yourself, take personal responsibility for your attitude and actions and find yourself even more committed to your spouse! Whether you've been married 5 months, 5 years or 50 years, there are ways you can renew your marriage and make it even better. Here are a few ideas on how to recharge your relationship and stay committed to each other.

Spend an evening dreaming together! That's right, spend an entire afternoon or evening making a list of activities and adventures you'd like to experience with your spouse. In the space below, make a list of the things you discover about the dreams you both share.

_____

_____

_____

_____

_____

What steps can you take to ensure some of those dreams come true?

_____

_____

_____

_____

Develop a plan to keep your love alive. If you wait to feel the emotion of love, you may have to wait a long time. But if you make the decision to love and choose to love in countless little ways every day, love can't help but come alive in your heart! In the space below, make a list of things you can do to help keep the love alive in your marriage.

_____

_____

_____

_____

_____

Seek God together on a regular basis. When was the last time you prayed, really prayed, with your spouse? Set aside time to get together on a regular basis to share what you're reading and discovering in the Bible. And don't forget to look for opportunities to pray together throughout the day—while you're riding in the car, taking a walk or simply sitting on the couch together. In the space below, make a list of ways you and your spouse can connect spiritually and grow in your relationship with God.

_____

_____

_____

_____

_____

Four Steps to Developing a Healthy Relationship

Gary and I believe that there are four steps to developing a healthy relationship! These steps are essential to growing together for a lifetime:

Step 1: *Encourage your mate and build him or her up.* Read Romans 14:19. What does Paul command the Romans to do?

_____

_____

_____

_____

Why is this so important to remember in daily life and in marriage?

_____

_____

_____

_____

Read 1 Thessalonians 5:11. What does Paul command the Thessalonians to do?

_____

_____

_____

_____

Why is this so important to remember in daily life and in marriage?

_____

_____

_____

_____

It's easy to forget the power of encouraging words. They breathe life and hope into people's hearts.

Step 2: Pray for your spouse. Never underestimate the power of prayer. We've seen hundreds of marriages on the brink of divorce come alive with joy, passion and new life because of the power of prayer. Read Hebrews 4:16. What promise is expressed in this verse in regard to prayer?

_____

_____

_____

_____

_____

Read Matthew 7:7. What promise is expressed in this verse in regard to prayer?

_____

_____

_____

_____

_____

There will be times when you will grow discouraged when it comes to unanswered prayer. Jesus knew these times would come. Read Luke 18:1-8. Why did Jesus tell the disciples this parable (see v. 1)?

_____

_____

_____

_____

_____

Why do you think it's important to be persistent in prayer?

_____

_____

_____

_____

You have the opportunity to take your spouse before God in prayer every day. It's never too late to begin praying!

Step 3: Ask God to let change begin with you. Marriages are renewed and restored when one person is willing to say to God, "Lord, let the change begin with me." One of the ways you can allow the change to begin with you is by taking a character assessment. In the space below, make a list of Christlike qualities that you'd like to see further developed in your life:

_____

_____

_____

_____

_____

Now identify some Scriptures for each character trait. For example, honesty might be represented by John 3:19-21, or generosity might be represented by Proverbs 11:25. Here are a few you may want to consider: faith (see Hebrews 11:1), forgiveness (see Matthew 5:44-45), fruitfulness (see John 15:8), contentment (see Proverbs 16:8), hope (see Colossians 1:27), humility (see Matthew 23:12), joy (see 1 Peter 1:8), love (see 1 John 2:10), compassion (see Isaiah 30:18), patience (see Galatians 6:9) and peace (see John 14:27).

Christlike Quality	Bible Reference
_____	_____
_____	_____
_____	_____
_____	_____
_____	_____
_____	_____

Reflecting on this list, what are some specific steps you can take to grow in each Christlike quality you listed?

_____

_____

_____

_____

_____

Use the Scripture as a means to measure your success. And don't forget to pray! Remember that the persistent prayers of the righteous change things (see James 5:16).

Retake the Great Expectations Quiz
In the first session, we asked you to take the Great Expectations Quiz. Now we'd like to challenge you to take it again *to see if your expectations have changed as you've completed this study.* On a scale of 1 to 10, place a number on the left side of the statement that represents what you expected in your marriage in this area. On a scale of 1 to 10, on the right side of the statement rank your experience in your marriage.

As you reflect on this list, did any of the scoring of your expectations change during this study? Explain in the space below.

_____

_____

_____

_____

_____

Did any of your scores remain the same? Explain in the space below.

_____

_____

_____

_____

Obviously, some scores didn't need to change, because they were already on target and healthy. But other scores may have shifted so that your expectations became healthier. These are the ones we want you to focus on. In what areas have you developed healthier expectations of your spouse? Of yourself? Of your marriage?

_____

_____

_____

_____

_____

_____

What you Hoped For	Expectation	What you Got
	1. We will have children. (If unable to have children, imagine the hurt and pain of a woman who wants to be a mom and her husband who wants to be a father.)	
	2. We will have many children.	
	3. We will have few children.	
	4. Long walks on the beach. (We will walk for no other purpose but connecting. Just me and my spouse, with the sand between our toes, our pants legs rolled up and the tide coming in.)	
	5. He will be a spiritual leader. (We will pray together, have daily devotions and attend church regularly.)	
	6. She will know how to submit.	
	7. Regular church attenders.	
	8. Nice house. (Imagine a white picket fence, furniture and backyard garden or downtown loft. Maybe not necessarily your first home, but your home a few years down the road.)	
	9. Romantic vacations. (Cruises, beach houses or remote cabins in the Rockies. The honeymoon experience will happen at least once a year.)	
	10. Regular vacations. (My spouse will take time away from the job or career each year to devote a full week to our marriage and family.)	

WHAT YOU HOPED FOR	EXPECTATION	WHAT YOU GOT
	11. *Deep conversations. (While dating, we spent hours on the phone. There will never come a day when I sense he is "rushing" me off the phone. My spouse will always love the sound of my voice.)*	
	12. *Bragging on each other in public. (While dating, we talked each other up to family and friends and showed each other's picture every chance we got. This will continue throughout our marriage.)*	
	13. *Courtesy. (Opening doors, pushing back a chair, offering a jacket on a cold night.)*	
	14. *Kindness. (We will always exchange uplifting, positive words in our communication.)*	
	15. *Give up friends. (I know that once we get married, my spouse will no longer have a desire to spend prolonged periods of time with friends. Hanging out with me will trump hanging out with friends.)*	
	16. *Time with friends. (My spouse will let me enjoy plenty of time with my friends. After all, we need relationships outside of the marriage to make life rich.)*	
	17. *Great eye contact. (When I speak, everything will stop because what I have to say will be treasured. My spouse will remove all distractions and focus on me.)*	
	18. *Hand holding. (We will hold hands at all times, in the movies, in the car, at the mall, during church and even at home.)*	
	19. *Patience. (We will never grow tired of repeating ourselves when the other person does not understand what we are saying.)*	
	20. *Dress up for dates and special nights. (My spouse will always put some thought into what he/she is wearing when we date.)*	

WHAT YOU HOPED FOR	EXPECTATION	WHAT YOU GOT
	21. We won't change. (Our personalities and passion will not fade or change with time.)	
	22. Dates. (From eating out to movies, we will have a regular date night that nothing interferes with.)	
	23. The "I'm glad to see you" look. (When we get home from work, there will always be an overwhelming response of elation to being in each other's presence.)	
	24. Media will not consume our time. (Our television viewing will be limited to a show/sporting event or two a week.)	
	25. Freedom from addiction. (Substance abuse, alcohol, pornography will not destroy our marriage.)	
	26. Unconditional love. (My spouse will love me even when I am going through difficult times emotionally.)	
	27. Physical health. (We will remain healthy throughout our marriage. Caring for each other through major illness will not be necessary.)	
	28. Tenderness/gentleness. (Our words will defuse anger and encourage each other.)	
	29. Validation. (My spouse will always understand my fear, frustration or hurt. Listening to me will always triumph over trying to solve my problems.)	
	30. Together forever. (We will never leave each other. The "D" word—divorce—will never be an option for us. We are together until one of us lays the other in the arms of Jesus.)	

WHAT YOU HOPED FOR	EXPECTATION	WHAT YOU GOT
	31. Snuggling on the couch. (Movie nights with popcorn will be a regular occurrence. Sometimes we will just snuggle with nothing to watch on TV. Just enjoying each other's presence will be enough.)	
	32. Sharing feelings. (I will always know my spouse's dreams, goals, hurts, hang-ups and frustrations. I will never have the need to guess, because there will always be a free flow of information.)	
	33. Grace and forgiveness. (The spirit of forgiveness will always exist in our home. We will not judge because we each are imperfect and make mistakes. There will be plenty of room for error.)	
	34. Devotions and prayer. (We will have a regular, daily quiet time with each other. We will work through the Bible, a book or devotional. We will pray at every meal.)	
	35. Cleanliness. (My spouse will always maintain a clean space, be it the closet, office, family room or bedroom. My spouse will always pick up and clean up his/her stuff.)	
	36. Closeness vs. close by. (We will always have a connectedness. We will never have the "in the same room, but checked out mentally" home.)	
	37. Humor/lightness. (We will never take ourselves too seriously. We know when to lighten up and when to laugh at ourselves.)	
	38. Servant, butler or maid. (We will cherish the opportunities to serve one another. We will always be that couple that refills an empty glass or picks up the dirty clothes of the other. Without hesitation or frustration we will look for opportunities to serve each other.)	

WHAT YOU HOPED FOR	EXPECTATION	WHAT YOU GOT
	39. Home-cooked meals. (*My spouse will have the table set, dinner on the stove and even, at times, candles lit. Dinner out or ordered in will be infrequent. Meals will be as good as [or better than] my mom's.*)	
	40. Understanding of work pressure. (*We will work hard to give each other space at the end of a long day.*)	
	41. Appreciation for work, job and career. (*My spouse will show interest in what I do and what I contribute to the family's bottom line.*)	
	42. Eyes for no other; faithfulness. (*My spouse's "eyes" do not wander off of me and onto another.*)	
	43. Ease of the words "I'm sorry." (*Remember when you were first dating? When you would offend one another, not only did the apology come easily, but often it was repeated.*)	
	44. Admission of mistakes. (*My spouse will always be forthcoming with mistakes and character defects in his/her life.*)	
	45. Appreciation for hobbies. (*I will have no problem with the time required for my spouse's hobbies, and my spouse will have no problem with mine.*)	
	46. Cared for when sick. (*Did he or she prepare get-well baskets stuffed with tissue, soup, candles or a favorite magazine? That kindness will continue throughout our marriage.*)	
	47. United front. (*No one will ever be able to put me down to my mate. No parent, family member or friend would get away with slandering me to him/her.*)	
	48. Protection. (*My spouse will take a bullet for me if necessary. Sounds in the middle of the night will be quickly investigated and resolved.*)	

WHAT YOU HOPED FOR	EXPECTATION	WHAT YOU GOT
	49. Companion. (We will love doing things together. We will never be one of those couples that go their separate way at movies, the mall or even at church.)	
	50. Sleeping together. (We will never sleep in separate rooms.)	
	51. Sex every day. (Regular sex will solve any lust problems.)	
	52. Creative sex. (Now I have the context to explore my sexual fantasies.)	
	53. Quickies. (She will serve me even when she is not in the mood.)	
	54. Sex all night. (We will make love until the sun comes up. Multiple orgasms will be experienced often.)	
	55. Family. (We will love each other's family and friends.)	
	56. Fondness of parents. (We will both get along well with our parents.)	
	57. Mom and Dad. (My spouse will like to hang around my mom and dad.)	
	58. Family history. (My spouse will show compassion for my family history.)	

What you Hoped For	Expectation	What you Got
	59. Accepting my family. (We will not judge or be critical of the actions of each other's family.)	
	60. Time with extended family. (My spouse will love spending a lot of time with my family members.)	
	61. In-law visits once or twice a year. (Mom and Dad will be able to set healthy boundaries without us needing to tell them. Visits will be minimal to help us "leave and cleave.")	
	62. Family holidays. (My spouse will have no problem with my family taking control of the holidays.)	
	63. Family traditions. (My spouse will happily honor my family traditions around the holidays.)	
	64. Decisions. (My spouse will have no problem seeing things from my point of view.)	
	65. One family income. (My spouse will make plenty of money to cover our expenses so I can stay home with the kids.)	
	66. Financial responsibility. (My mate will hold down a good job, make a good living and provide for the needs of the home.)	
	67. Financial security. (We will have plenty of money to do what we need to do as a family. We will be all about paying bills on time, keeping debt to a minimum and giving to charitable organizations.)	
	68. Financial freedom. (My spouse will have no problem spending money freely. We will not need to keep a tight rein on the checkbook.)	

WHAT YOU HOPED FOR	EXPECTATION	WHAT YOU GOT
	69. Tithing. (We will give a minimum of 10 percent of our income to our church.)	
	70. Savings. (We will spend less than 100 percent of what we make so we have some to put into savings.)	
	71. Giving. (Money will be set aside to give to charitable organizations beyond our tithing.)	
	72. Retirement. (We will have plenty of money saved up so that we can stop working at a reasonable age.)	
	73. Church denomination. (We will mutually agree on the denomination for our family. My spouse will not bash my denominational preference.)	
	74. Theology. (We will merge our beliefs and have few theological differences.)	
	75. Worship style. (We will enjoy the same kind of worship experience.)	
	76. Entertainment. (From music to movies, we will be able to find a happy medium that both of us can enjoy.)	
	77. Promptness. (We will both work to be at events and family gatherings on time.)	
	78. Physically fit. (We will live healthy lives. Excessive weight gain will not occur.)	

Our hope is that you've seen your expectations become more reasonable and healthy over the course of this study as you've discovered what makes you and your spouse tick, and you've made some adjustments. Our prayer for you is that your marriage will continue to grow stronger and be full of love and joy for years to come.

Taking It with You

No matter what has happened in your marriage, it's never too late to do the work to save your relationship. Forgiving a moral failure or addiction is challenging, but it's not a challenge that can't be overcome. Remember, you are 100 percent responsible for your actions, not the actions of your spouse. That means you have the freedom to choose to forgive. It's not an easy decision, and it does not condone the behavior or action. But it will set you free to love and trust again and experience the healing and restoration that only come from knowing God.

Put It into Practice

Choose at least one of these suggested activities below to complete over the next week. Consider sharing with your friends or small-group members the impact it has on you and your relationship with your spouse.

I. Review the Q&A sections in *As Long as We Both Shall Live*

Which questions can you most relate to? Do you have any questions for Gary and Ted? If so, go online to the Smalley Relationship Center at www.smalleyonline.com and submit a question. Each week one question is selected and answered.

2. Read Song of Solomon Aloud with Your Spouse This Week
Dive into this passionate book of the Bible with your spouse and explore its meaning. While reading, look at the portrait God has drawn of a man and woman in love. Talk about what you learn with your spouse.

3. Memorize a Scripture Passage
This week, commit the following Scripture to memory: "Until now you have not asked for anything in my name. Ask and you will receive, and your joy will be complete" (John 16:24).

LEADER'S GUIDE

Session I
THE EXPECTATIONS OF MARRIAGE
Chapter I in *As Long as We Both Shall Live*

For Starters

Think of several expectations about marriage that you can look back on and laugh about when you think of them now. In the space below, describe three of those expectations you no longer have. Answers will vary but may include things like thinking your spouse would wake up with minty fresh breath every morning, be excited and energetic to have sex five times a day or be able to balance family and work with ease!

Think of several expectations about marriage that you had on your wedding day and still have today. In the space below, list three of them. Answers will vary, but expectations for marital faithfulness, great communication, a healthy sex life and the ability to have fun together may be among those mentioned.

What is the difference between the expectations you now consider as silly and those you consider as reasonable and timeless? How would your marriage be different if you held on firmly to those silly expectations? How would your marriage be different if you let go of those reasonable expectations? Answers will vary, but the difference between silly and reasonable expectations is often a matter of experience. After being married for a few weeks, months and even years, the more colorful, outrageous expectations often fall to the wayside. Holding on to "silly" expectations as well as letting go of reasonable expectations can undermine a marriage.

Discussion and Study

Can you think of any healthy expectations that can help strengthen a marriage . . . other than the ones described in the paragraph above? Describe those expectations in the space below. Answers will vary but may include the expectation that my spouse will be honest with me; my spouse will display common courtesy to me; and my spouse will honor me.

Can you think of any unhealthy expectations that can undermine a marriage? Describe them in the space below. Answers will vary, but whenever a spouse expects perfection or expects the other person to "always" do so and so, it can lead to trouble. No one is perfect. Mistakes happen. And there must be grace for one another.

Think about an expectation you had early in your relationship that went unmet. How did you respond? In the space below make a list of some of the emotions you felt as a direct response to your unmet expectation. Answers will vary.

How did you resolve the issue of unmet expectations in this area of your marriage? Or has it remained unresolved? Explain in the space below. Answers will vary.

Read Genesis 29:1-11. How did Jacob respond to meeting Rachel (see vv. 10-11)? When Jacob saw Rachel, he was taken by her. He immediately served the young shepherdess by removing the stone from the mouth of the well so she could water her flocks. Then he walked up to her and kissed her and wept!

Though the Scripture does not specifically say, what do you think was going through Jacob's mind, heart and emotions during his first encounter with Rachel (see vv. 10-11)? Answers will vary, but it's fair to suggest that Jacob was smitten by Rachel. He took the first opportunity to serve her by helping move the stone to water the flocks. Then he kissed her—a sign of affection—and began crying. This was a man who could not hold back his emotions. He probably felt excitement, joy, hope and a bit twitterpated.

Read Genesis 29:12-20. What was Laban's response to Jacob? Laban's response was gracious and kind. He embraced Jacob, kissed him and brought him into his house. He invited Jacob to stay with him a month and then agreed to give Rachel to him in marriage for seven years of service.

Following Laban's initial response, what do you think some of Jacob's expectations were regarding his relationship with Rachel? Though the Scripture does not list all of Jacob's expectations, it's fair to estimate that he was imagining his life with his bride-to-be. Seven years is a long time to wait for the one you love, but Jacob did it with grace and strength. He had years to build all kinds of expectations regarding where they would live and their life together.

Read Genesis 29:21-26. How did Laban deceive Jacob? After seven long years of service, Jacob didn't give his promised daughter, Rachel, but instead gave his eldest daughter, Leah. Laban broke his promise.

How do you think Jacob's expectations regarding marriage were affected? All of his expectations were destroyed in that moment. Jacob had painted a picture of what his life with Rachel would look like and only when it was too late did he realize that he had been given a completely different portrait.

Read Genesis 29:27-30. How did Laban offer to resolve the situation? Do you think the offer was fair? Why or why not? Why do you think Laban tricked Jacob? Laban offered to give Rachel to Jacob for another seven years of service. The offer was not fair, because Laban had tricked Jacob so he could get seven more years of service out of the young man.

Read Genesis 29:31-35. After Jacob married Rachel, what kind of unexpected conflict arose in their marriage? Rachel was unable to have children, yet Leah was able to give Jacob children.

In what ways has your life turned out different from what you expected? How has this affected your attitude toward your spouse? Your family? Your marriage? Answers will vary.

The Great Expectations Quiz. This quiz is also in the first chapter of the book and it's an important one for spouses to take because it highlights the expectations that each of us carries into marriage, and the gap between those expectations and our experiences.

Read Genesis 30:25-43; 31:1-2. Why was Laban at odds with Jacob? Laban didn't want to let Jacob and his family go because Laban recognized that God's blessing was on Jacob's life, which poured over onto his own life.

What happened to Laban's attitude toward Jacob (see v. 2)? Laban was no longer friendly toward Jacob.

Read Genesis 31:1-21. How did God intervene in the situation (see vv. 3,9,11-12,16)? God provided specific instruction for Jacob to return to the land of his fathers. God also blessed Jacob with livestock. He spoke to Jacob in a dream with specific instruction. He gave Jacob favor with his wives to leave their homeland.

Read Genesis 31:22-55. How do things turn out for Jacob and his family? Laban finally agrees to let his daughters go, and Jacob is able to return to his homeland.

Session 2
DEEP ROOTS AND CULTURAL INFLUENCES
Chapters 2–3 in *As Long as We Both Shall Live*

For Starters

Spend a few moments thinking about your childhood and your family. What are three things you loved about the way you were raised that you'd like to give to your own children? Describe in the space below. Answers will vary.

Can you think of one thing you'd do differently in raising your own children? Describe. Answers will vary.

In what specific ways do you think our culture influences the way you think about marriage and family? Do you think those influences are primarily healthy, unhealthy or benign? Explain. Answers will vary.

Discussion and Study

Now place a check by the one that best describes your spouse.

____ The Dominant Parent   ____ The Neglectful Parent

____ The Permissive Parent   ____ The Loving and Firm Parent

How has that experience shaped you? How has it shaped your spouse? Answers will vary.

How has that experience shaped your expectations of marriage and family? Your spouse's expectations of marriage and family? Answers will vary.

How have your roots affected the way you're growing into a spouse, parent and follower of Christ? How have your spouse's roots affected him or her in these roles? Answers will vary.

Read Exodus 20:12. What commandment is highlighted in this verse? Honor your father and mother.

According to the second half of the verse, why is it so important to follow this commandment? What happens to someone who refuses to honor his or her father and mother? Honoring your father and mother extends your time in the place God has for you. It can be estimated that you cannot move into the fullness of what God has for you if you do not honor your parents.

Have you ever known someone whose unresolved relationship with his or her mother or father actually seemed to hold the person back in life? If so, explain. Answers will vary.

Is there anything in the past with your own relationship with your mom or dad that needs to be forgiven so that you can move forward into the "land which the Lord your God gives you" (Exodus 20:12)? Explain. Answers will vary.

As you look at the list of generation styles below, which describes you? Now place a checkmark by the one that best describes your spouse.

   ___ The Builder Generation   ___ The Boomer Generation
   ___ The Buster Generation   ___ The Bridger Generation

In what ways has the generation you were born into shaped your expectations for marriage? Your expectations for raising a family? Answers will vary.

What is your favorite romantic movie? Why is it your favorite? What about the plot, the storyline or the characters do you love the most? Answers will vary.

Think about the perfect marriage. What popular song would you select as a theme song for that marriage? Answers will vary.

What book have you read recently that best describes what a great marriage looks like? Answers will vary.

What cultural element—music, television, movies, books, the Internet, theater most influences the way you think about marriage and family? Answers will vary.

Do you think it's important to focus your time and energy on shows, movies and music that offer a healthy view of marriage? Why or why not? Answers will vary, but focusing on those things that are good and healthy can encourage people to build stronger, longer lasting relationships.

In the space below, write the words of Philippians 4:8: "Finally, brothers, whatever is true, whatever is noble, whatever is right, whatever is pure, whatever is lovely, whatever is admirable—if anything is excellent or praiseworthy—think about such things."

In the space below, write the words of Psalm 119:37: "Turn my eyes away from worthless things; preserve my life according to your word."

Read Isaiah 33:14-16. According to this passage, what is required of the person who is to dwell with God (v. 15)? The person will walk righteously and speak what is right, reject gain from extortion and keep from accepting bribes, stop his or her ears against plots of murder, and shut his or her eyes against contemplating evil.

What is promised to the person who does those things (see v. 16)? The person will dwell on the heights, his or her refuge will be the mountain fortress, his or her bread will be supplied, and water will not fail him or her.

Chorus No. 1: "It's Mine, All Mine"
Chorus No. 2: "It's All About Me"

Chorus No. 3: "If It Feels Good, Do It"
Chorus No. 4: "To Each His Own"

Of those four choruses, which are you most susceptible to "singing"? Answers will vary. You may want to ask a follow-up question to find out if there's any link between the chorus a person is most susceptible to and the generation in which he or she was born.

Which one is most likely to undermine your marriage? Answers will vary.

What can you do to protect your marriage, your spouse and your family from falling prey to these cultural choruses? Answers will vary but may include spending time in the Scriptures, prayer, fellowship with other believers and godly mentors.

Session 3
PERSONALITY PLAY AND
UNPACKING PAST RELATIONSHIPS
Chapters 4–5 in *As Long as We Both Shall Live*

For Starters
Make a list of three things you absolutely love and appreciate about your spouse. Then make a list of three things you wish you could change about your spouse.

LOVE AND APPRECIATE	WISH YOU COULD CHANGE

Now take a step back and look at your lists. Which entries are linked to personality differences? Answers will vary, but often the things we love and appreciate as well as the things that drive us nuts about our spouse are linked to personality traits. For instance, a spouse who is loving and laid back may also have a tendency to be late and lose track of time. Or a spouse who is the life of the party may not be able to organize things or keep track of details. Often there is a strong link between the things we love about a person and the things that drive us crazy.

Do you see any connection between your spouse's greatest strengths and greatest weaknesses? Do you see any connection between your own strengths and weaknesses? Answers will vary, but often the greatest strengths and weaknesses are linked. A well-organized administrative type personality may not be the most flexible or spontaneous. Meanwhile, a driven leader-oriented type personality may have a tough time unplugging from work and relaxing.

Discussion and Study
How does it make you feel to know that God created your "inmost being" and knitted you together in your mother's womb? Answers will vary, but knowing that we are made by God should give us a sense of worth, value and affirmation. It should make us want to worship and give thanks to God even more.

Do you believe that God did a good job when He made you? Why or why not? Answers will vary, but you may be surprised with how many people really struggle with this truth. They don't see themselves as fashioned beautifully by God.

Is there anything that prevents you from accepting the truth that you are "fearfully and wonderfully made"? If so explain. Answers will vary, but when we don't believe the truth of what the Scripture says about us, then we will eventually become convinced of things that simply aren't true. These untruths will short-circuit all that God wants to do in our lives.

Do you feel like you know the truth of Psalm 139:13-14 "full well"? Why or why not? Answers will vary. This is a passage worth committing to memory.

As you look at the list of personality types below, which describes you? Now place a checkmark by the one that best describes your spouse.

____ The Precise Personality

____ The Pleaser Personality

____ The Party Personality

____ The Powerful Personality

Answers will vary, but most couples will find that they do not share the same personality type. When it comes to specific advice for getting along with a personality that is different from your own, we highly encourage you to read the chapter "Personality Play and Unpacking Past Relationships" in *As Long as We Both Shall Live.*

In what ways does your personality complement your spouse's personality? Answers will vary, but generally couples will find that one person's weakness is another person's strength, and vice versa. In areas where couples share strengths, they can do amazing things when working together.

In what ways does your personality create opportunities for conflict with your spouse's personality? Answers will vary, but every difference is an opportunity for conflict or celebration. We believe that God meant you to celebrate the differences and learn to appreciate all that is possible through Him as you learn to live, love and serve together.

What changes can you make to help strengthen the communication, compassion and understanding when it comes to personality differences in your marriage? This introspective question is designed to force readers to reflect on the changes they need to make. This highlights part of the next section of the progression—personal responsibility.

Read Luke 10:38-42. How did Martha respond to Jesus' visit? Martha welcomed Jesus. She went out of her way to make sure everything was in order for His visit. She was busy preparing the food and presumably the house for the special visit. She was task oriented and focused.

How did Mary respond to Jesus' visit? The Scripture doesn't say that Mary greeted Jesus like her sister did. Instead, she sat at the Lord's feet listening to His every word. Even when she was rebuked by her sister, she did not respond or try to defend herself. Instead, she let Jesus respond for her.

Reflecting on the four personality types—Precise, Pleaser, Party and Powerful—which would you say best describes Martha? Martha exhibits traits of the Powerful Personality. She is task-oriented and a natural leader. She was willing to do what it took to get things organized for the meal with Jesus. She also displayed some characteristics of the Precise Personality. She was quick to criticize Mary and saw the situation in black or white terms. Her sister needed to help.

Which would you say best describes Mary? Mary exhibited traits of the Pleaser Personality. She was warm and accepting of Jesus' presence and a great listener.

Read John 11:1-37. What caused the sisters to send a message to Jesus (see John 11:1)? Their brother, Lazarus, was very sick. They sent word so that Jesus would know.

Upon Jesus' arrival, what did He discover (see John 11:17)? Lazarus had been in the tomb for four days.

How does Martha display her faith in her interaction with Jesus (see John 11:21-27)? Martha went out to meet Jesus, but Mary stayed home. As a Powerful Personality, Martha was the first to step up to the plate to greet Jesus. She was a natural leader and go-getter. She wanted to be with her Lord. Mary was more of a Pleaser Personality and thus more reserved. She stayed back and waited for Jesus to come to her.

How does Martha display her faith in her interaction with Jesus (see John 11:21-27)? Martha acknowledges that Jesus' delay played a role in her brother's death. She had seen Jesus heal others and knew He had the ability to heal him. But her faith went one step further when she said, "But I know that even now God will give you whatever you ask" (John 11:22). Indeed, Martha was a woman of great faith, courage and strength. And her Powerful Personality was an asset to her relationship with Jesus.

How did Mary respond to the invitation of Jesus (see v. 29)? She got up quickly and went to Him.

What was Mary's response to Jesus compared to Martha's (see John 11:21-22,32)? How did the differences in their responses reflect their personalities? Mary's initial response to Jesus was very similar to Martha's. Both acknowledged that if Jesus had come sooner, Lazarus would not have died. While Mary ended her statement in tears, Martha ended hers in the faith-filled proclamation, "But I know that even now God will give you whatever you ask." Mary's Pleaser Personality only challenged Jesus to a certain point, while Martha's Powerful Personality challenged Jesus with the truth that nothing was impossible for Him.

Read John 11:28-43. How would the story have been different if only Mary or Martha were present? How is the story and the faith journey of all strengthened by the presence of Mary and Martha? Different personalities illuminate different aspects of the wonder of God. Through Mary we see the contemplative, peaceful personality at play. Through Martha we see the strong, leadership personality at play. Through their interactions with Jesus—which were different—we better understand who He was and His work in the middle of a terrible situation.

Read Ecclesiastes 4:7-12. According to this passage, what are some of the benefits of being with someone else? When you're alone, there's a tendency to work too much. Even though you accumulate much, there's no one to share it with and enjoy the fruit of your labor with. Two are better than one because there is more to enjoy together. When times are tough, there's someone to pick you up. When times are cold, there is someone to keep you warm. When times are treacherous, there is someone to help protect and defend you. If the "third cord" is God in your relationship—how much stronger are you as a couple!

Read Romans 15:7. What is the result of accepting your spouse just as he or she is? You bring praise to God! In other words, God is pleased when you honor others!

Read Matthew 7:1-5. What instruction is given toward judging others? Don't do it!

Why do you think it's easier to see the speck of sawdust in someone else's eye rather than the plank of wood in your own? Sometimes we don't really want to see our own weaknesses or faults. It's easier to focus our energy on someone else rather than ourselves.

Read Proverbs 12:18. What wisdom does this verse offer for moments of tension in marriage?

Speaking rashly can bring harm. But wise words will bring healing to the situation and the relationship.

Read Ephesians 4:2. What attitude should you have as you deal with misunderstandings? We should have the attitude of Christ. Be completely humble and gentle; be patient, bearing with one another in love

Session 4
EXPECTING THE BEST AND EXTRAVAGANT LOVE
Chapters 6–7 in *As Long as We Both Shall Live*

For Starters
In the space below, make a list of three expectations you brought to marriage that have the widest gap between what you expected and what you have experienced in your relationship with your spouse.

1. _____

2. _____

3. _____

Answers will vary but may include things like financial responsibility or communication-related expectations.

Do you think your expectations are fair and reasonable? Why or why not? Answers will vary. Most people will tend to defend their expectations even if they are unreasonable.

If you expressed each of the three expectations to your spouse, do you think your spouse would find them reasonable? Why or why not? Answers will vary. Generally speaking, expectations that include the word "always," "never," or "every time" are the hardest to meet. In addition, expectations that are extremely general are also difficult. It's much easier to meet an expectation when it's more specific.

Discussion and Study
In the space below make a list of the expectations you've brought into your marriage that you still hold on to even though they have gone unmet. Prayerfully ask the Holy Spirit to expose your expectations—those spoken and unspoken. Answers will vary. This question should be treated tenderly and with much grace.

Now you need to address each expectation one at a time. Prayerfully ask God to reveal where these expectations came from and whether or not they are reasonable to keep. Are there any adjustments you need to make to your list of expectations to make them more attainable? If so, make a list of your newly modified expectations below: Again, answers will vary, but if addressing this question in a group, proceed prayerfully and gently.

Now reviewing your original list again, are there any expectations that you need to eliminate completely? If so, write them below and then draw a line through each one, symbolically marking it out. Then spend time in prayer asking God to change your heart regarding this expectation. Some expectations are simply unfair or overly demanding. For example, expecting your spouse to make over $10 million a year is unreasonable if not impossible. But many of the expectations may be just unreasonable, especially if we are asking our spouses to give us something they simply do not have.

Finally, take another look at your original list. Are there any expectations that are unreasonable or unbiblical? Open your Bible and read 1 Corinthians 13. Do each of your expectations fit within the guidelines of this Scripture passage? If so, write the remaining expectations below. Answers will vary, but all of our expectations should fit within the guidelines of Scripture.

Read Romans 8:35-40. In the space below, make a list of the things that will try to separate you from the love of Christ. Tribulation, distress, persecution, famine, nakedness, peril and sword. In addition, death, life, angels, principalities, things present, things to come, powers, height, depth, nor any other created thing can separate us from the love of God which is in Christ Jesus our Lord.

What is the promise given to the children of God during these trials (see v. 37)? In all these things we will overwhelmingly conquer through Him who loved us.

Second Corinthians 5:14-17 says, "For the love of Christ controls us, having concluded this, that one died for all, therefore all died; and He died for all, so that they who live might no longer live for themselves, but for Him who died and rose again on their behalf. Therefore from now on we recognize no one according to the flesh; even though we have known Christ according to the flesh, yet now we know Him in this way no longer. Therefore if anyone is in Christ, he is a new creature; the old things passed away; behold, new things have come" (NASB). According to this passage, how are we changed when the love of Christ controls us? We no longer live for ourselves with selfish tendencies, but instead we live to honor God. We are made into new creatures. The old things pass away and we are made new.

Read Mark 14:1-9. What was some of the criticism the woman received for her outrageous gift? Some people criticized her gift as a waste while others thought it would have been more practical to give the money to the poor.

What was Jesus' response to the gift (see vv. 6-9)? Jesus defends the woman and her outrageous generosity. He points out that the woman was doing something incredibly significant—anointing the man for His own burial. As a result of her extravagant love, she would be remembered for ages to come. Your reading of this passage is a fulfillment of that promise.

What is a righteous response to extravagant acts of love? Answers will vary, but acknowledgement, respect, gratitude and thankfulness are appropriate responses.

Is there anything that prevents you from being more extravagant in the way you display love? Explain. Answers will vary but may include unawareness, fear and self-centeredness. In addition, it's hard to love extravagantly when you don't know just how extravagantly you're loved by God.

What actions, words and attitudes make your spouse feel truly loved? Answers will vary but may include things like spending time together, gifts, acts of service and words of affirmation. Cleaning up the house unexpectedly, giving a spouse time to hang with friends or complete a project or simply cuddling together on the couch may be things that make your spouse feel really loved.

What are some specific ways you can express extravagant love to your spouse this week? Answers will vary, but this question is designed to encourage specific acts of love and service.

What kind words does your spouse really need to hear? It may have been weeks, months or years since you grabbed your spouse, looked him or her in the eye and said how much you really love and appreciate him or her as a child of God, friend, lover and spouse. How can you express with fresh words and meaning the value of your spouse? What can you say? Specifically high-light your spouse's good qualities by name. Go ahead—make a long list!

What kind words do you need to hear from your spouse? This question is de-signed to be more personal and introspective. What affirming words do you long to hear? What words of affirmation bring you to life and give you energy and hope?

What kind of encouragement does your spouse really need right now? How can you provide it? This question is designed to challenge you to take a big-picture perspective on your spouse's life right now. Is there discouragement at work, home or in your spouse's spiritual life? How can you catch your spouse doing something right?

What kind of encouragement do you need right now that your spouse can provide? Be specific in your response. When you can let your spouse know exactly what you need to hear—even the wording—you're more likely to get it! Sometimes spouses need to be coached on how to meet needs.

Session 5
THE SERVANT AND COMMITTED FOREVER
Chapters 8–9 in *As Long as We Both Shall Live*

For Starters

Why do you think it's so important to maintain a servant's heart in a marriage? Why do you think it's so easy to lose a servant's heart? Answers will vary, but it's es-sential to maintain a servant's heart for the health of a marriage. One sig-nificant way of expressing love is through acts of kindness and service. When we do things for each other and care for one another, then we nat-urally nurture each other.

What are some of the lifelong goals you share with your spouse? Answers will vary but may include children, grandchildren, retirement, home ownership, travel and work, among others.

What activities do you and your spouse do that highlight your commitment to one another? These may include a wide variety of activities, including dreaming about a future together.

Discussion and Study

Read John 13:1-17. Why was this evening so significant to Jesus and the disciples (see vv. 1-5)? It was important because it was before the Passover feast. He was about to be betrayed by Judas, and He knew His time with the disciples was coming to a close. This passage highlights one of His most important symbolic acts.

What did Jesus do when He got up from the meal (see vv. 4-5)? What symbolism was displayed in His actions? Jesus took off his outer clothing, assuming a more humble position, and wrapped a towel around His waist like a servant. He poured water into a basin and began washing His disciples' feet and dried them with the very towel He was wearing. The act was incredibly vulnerable and intimate. Jesus symbolically took on the role of a servant. He tenderly washed the feet of each of His disciples—representing His involvement in their lives. Some may argue that the act also symbolized the washing that would happen through His sacrifice—that sins would be washed away. The act was very personal, unusual and special.

Why do you think Simon Peter protested Jesus' action (see vv. 6-9)? Answers will vary, but initially Peter didn't understand the importance of what Jesus was doing.

What lesson did Jesus want to teach His disciples through His actions (see vv. 12-17)? Jesus wanted to teach His disciples that loving God meant loving each other. It meant getting into the grit and grime of each other's lives and helping each other. It meant having a servant's heart no matter what title you may earn.

In what ways do you "wash your spouse's feet" (serve your spouse) on a regular basis? Answers will vary but may include offering more affirming words on a regular basis, volunteering for particular chores around the house or looking for ways to spend time together.

Are there any things you can do to be more intentional about washing the feet of your spouse on a daily basis? Answers will vary.

Are there any ways in which you're short-circuiting your spouse's efforts to serve you? Explain. Answers will vary, but sometimes all of us—like Peter—protest someone else's efforts to serve us. We may decline graciously, claim we don't have the need or simply refuse the offer. If left unchecked, this can become an unhealthy habit. Part of being a great servant and someone who is generous requires knowing how to receive graciously.

Read Matthew 10:42. What act of service is mentioned in this passage? Why is it so significant? Giving a cup of cold water to a child is highlighted as an act of service in this passage. It's significant because of its insignificance. In other words, giving someone a cup of cold water may seem like a mundane, everyday activity, but it carries eternal rewards.

Read Acts 20:18-19. What act of service is mentioned in this passage? Why is it so significant? Paul is acknowledging that he served his fellow followers of God by being with them faithfully.

Read Galatians 6:10. What act of service is mentioned in this passage? Why is it so significant? The act of service is simply doing good. That can be interpreted many ways, but the idea is that when we do good to others, it honors God.

Sometimes the issue of the roles that men and women fulfill in a marriage in regards to serving one another can cause conflict. Read Ephesians 5:22-33. Why do you think this passage can be so problematic for men and women? Many men and women feel uncomfortable with this passage. The word "submit" is often a barrier for many women and the idea of "laying down your life" seems unappealing to many men.

What instructions are wives given in Ephesians 5:22-24? Wives are to submit to their husbands as to the Lord. Just as the Church submits to Christ, so also wives should submit to their husbands.

What instructions are husbands given in Ephesians 5:25-30? Husbands are to love their wives just as Christ loved the Church and gave Himself up for it. Husbands are to love their wives as their own bodies, for he who loves his wife loves himself.

Which assignment do you think is more difficult: the instructions given to women or the instructions given to men? Explain. Answers will vary, but both men and women can build a convincing case that their side is more difficult.

What does it mean when the Bible says "two will become one flesh" (Ephesians 5:31)? It means that two will be united into one. In many ways this is a mystery that began with the first couple, Adam and Eve, described in the first three chapters of Genesis.

In what ways have you and your spouse "become one flesh"? Answers will vary, but the idea of becoming one flesh is much more than just sex. As a couple grows together, they find themselves able to complete each other's sentences, sometimes communicating without saying a word and even having the exact same thought or reaction without communicating.

Why do you think it's so important for a man to love his wife and a wife to respect her husband (see Ephesians 5:32)? While everyone needs to be loved and respected, women have a unique desire to be loved and men have a unique desire to be respected. If a woman feels unloved or a man does not feel respected, a marriage can sour quickly.

Why do you think Paul prescribes love for wives and respect for husbands? In what way have you found this prescription helpful in your own marriage? Answers will vary, but Paul noticed this distinction between men and women enough to mention it.

As you read through this list, were there any expectations that your spouse has met for you almost all the time? Describe in the space below. Answers will vary, but hopefully you'll have had your expectations met on most if not all of this list.

As you read through this list, were there any expectations that you need to revive in your marriage? Describe in the space below. You have let go of a particular expectation, but it may be right to revive it by communicating your desire to your spouse.

Are there any expectations that you'd like to add to the list? Describe in the space below. Answers will vary.

Read Psalm 145:18. What is God's commitment to you in this verse? If you call on the Lord in truth, He will be near to you.

Read Matthew 18:20. What is God's commitment to you in this verse? Where you and one to two others come together in His name, He will be with you.

Read Hebrews 13:5-6. What is God's commitment to you in these verses? He will never leave you or forsake you. He will be your helper, so you do not need to be afraid.

Read 1 Corinthians 10:13. What is God's commitment to you in this verse? God will not let you be tempted beyond what you can bear. But when you are tempted, He will also provide a way out for you so that you can stand up under that temptation.

Session 6
A FULFILLING MARRIAGE
Chapters 10–11 in *As Long as We Both Shall Live*

For Starters
List three "priceless moments" from your marriage. What made them so special? Answers will vary but may include the birth of a child, a special trip, a memorable anniversary celebration or treasured times of intimacy and connection.

Why do you think commitment is so foundational for a healthy marriage? Without commitment you don't have to work through issues, seek solutions or grow as individuals.

How does knowing that you and your spouse are committed to each other strengthen your relationship? It strengthens your will to fight for reconciliation and understanding.

Discussion and Study

In the space below, make a list of the things you discover about the dreams you both share. Answers will vary.

What practical steps can you take to ensure some of those dreams come true? Answers will vary.

In the space below, make a list of things you can do to help keep the love alive in your marriage. Answers will vary but may include words of affirmation, surprising acts of service or kindness or activities like leaving notes around the house.

In the space below, make a list of ways you and your spouse can connect spiritually and grow in your relationship with God. Answers will vary, but should include making it a priority to set aside time to connect as a couple. During this time, couples should make every effort to communicate with one another and really listen to each other.

Read Romans 14:19. What does Paul command the Romans to do? He commands them to make every effort to do what leads to peace and to mutual edification.

Why is this so important to remember in daily life and in marriage? Everyone needs to be encouraged. It's easy to get discouraged at work, by the media news or at the amount of work that has to get done each day. Kind words can go a long way toward fueling people to keep going even when they are tired and weary.

Read 1 Thessalonians 5:11. What does Paul command the Thessalonians to do? He commands them to encourage each another and build each other up.

Why is this so important to remember in daily life and in marriage? Because everyone needs encouragement. All too often our words tear people down rather than build them up. We need to be intentional about loving others.

Read Hebrews 4:16. What promise is expressed in this verse in regard to prayer? We can approach the throne of grace with confidence, know that we will receive grace and mercy in our time of need.

Read Matthew 7:7. What promise is expressed in this verse in regard to prayer? If we ask, it will be given to us. If we seek, we will find. If we knock, the door will be opened to us.

Read Luke 18:1-8. Why did Jesus tell the disciples this parable (see v. 1)? To show them they should always pray and not give up.

Why do you think it's important to be persistent in prayer? Because God answers prayer. He may not answer in the way we expect or the timing we prefer, but He is faithful in every situation.

One of the ways you can allow the change to begin with you is by taking a character assessment. In the space below, make a list of Christlike qualities that you'd like to see further developed in your life. Answers will vary but may include qualities like dependability, sincerity, big-heartedness, kindness or generosity.

Reflecting on this list, what are some specific steps you can take to grow in each Christlike quality you listed? Answers will vary.

As you reflect on this list, did any of the scoring of your expectations change during this study? Explain in the space below. Hopefully, they have been able to develop more reasonable, healthy expectations.

Did any of your scores remain the same? Explain in the space below. Answers will vary.

In what areas have you developed healthier expectations of your spouse? Of yourself? Of your marriage? Answers will vary.

twoignite

TWOPLAY,
TWOLAUGH,
& TWOHAVE FUN

created to strengthen marriage through action

twoignite.com
sponsored by TripFire.com

TWOPLAY, TWOLAUGH, & TWOHAVE FUN

*created to strengthen
marriage through action*

twoignite.com
sponsored by TripFire.com

GREAT EXPECTATIONS FOR LASTING LOVE

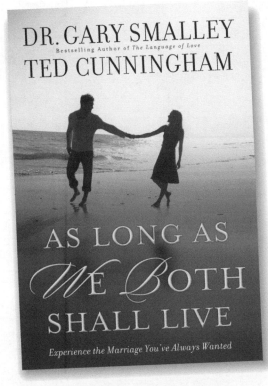

In marriage, undisclosed expectations can be dangerous. When couples expect each other to be and act a certain way without communicating their assumptions, disappointment is just around the corner! In *As Long as We Both Shall Live*, Gary Smalley and Ted Cunningham show you how to defuse the ticking time bomb of unrealistic expectations and deepen your relationship with honesty, empathy and respect. *As Long as We Both Shall Live* will help you and your spouse acknowledge your unexpressed assumptions, understand one another's genuine needs and talk openly about your hopes and desires. As you use the tools found in each chapter, you'll build a lasting, loving marriage and dream up a new picture of your life together!

As Long as We Both Shall Live
Gary Smalley and Ted Cunningham
ISBN: 08307.46803
ISBN: 978.08307.46804